Guitar Book for Adult Beginners

Teach Yourself How to Play Famous Guitar Songs, Guitar Chords, Theory & Technique

No Music Reading Required!

Damon Ferrante

Book & Streaming Video Lessons

Introduction: How the Book & Videos Work

As a music professor and guitar teacher for over twenty five years, I have wanted to help beginner guitar students succeed in playing songs and making progress. In the past, beginner guitar books have taken a dull and uninspiring approach. Most of the time these books just throw together songs and techniques in a random, boring, and confusing way; sometimes these books are no better than blurry photocopies.

This book and video course takes a new and innovative approach!

The Guitar Book for Adult Beginners makes learning famous guitar songs fun, easy, interactive, and engaging. The book and streaming videos follow a step-by-step lesson format for learning some of the most famous music. Songs you have always dreamt about playing on the guitar for yourself and for your family and friends!

In the *Guitar Book for Adult Beginners,* each lesson builds on the previous one in a clear and easy-to-understand manner. No music reading is necessary. I walk you through how to play these wonderful songs, starting with very easy music, at the beginning of the book, and advancing, little by little, as you master new repertoire and techniques. As you are able to play these new songs, you will also greatly improve your abilities on the guitar! Along the way, you will learn to read music, play chords and some scales, learn rhythms, techniques, and music theory, as well.

If you have always wanted to play the guitar, then, this book is for you. Let's get started on this exciting musical journey!

The Videos

> ❖**Check Out**
> **Video 1**

The symbol above means that there is a video lesson that corresponds to the material presented on the lesson page. These video lessons cover the concepts presented and also give instruction and tips on how to play certain songs pieces from the book.

To access the video lessons, go to steeplechasemusic.com and click on the link at the top of the page for Guitar Books. Then, from the Guitar Books webpage, click on the image for this book, "Guitar Book for Adult Beginners". On the webpage for the *Guitar Book for Adult Beginners*, you will see a link to Video Lessons. Click the link for the Video Lessons webpage for this book. The video lessons are free and there is no limit on the number of times you may watch them.

Here is a list of some of the Great Guitar Music that you will learn in this book:

- *Amazing Grace*
- *Happy Birthday*
- *House of the Rising Sun*
- *Scarborough Fair*
- *Shenandoah*
- *Take Me Out to the Ballgame*
- *Kum-Bah-Yah*
- *Jingle Bells*
- *Ode to Joy* by Beethoven
- *This Little Light of Mine*
- *Peace Like a River*
- *Silent Night*
- *Rockabilly*
- *When the Saints Go Marching In*
- *Greensleeves*
- *Aura Lee*
- *Blues*
- *Sometimes I Feel Like a Motherless Child*
- And Many More Songs and Pieces!

Table of Contents

GOOD NEWS!

This edition of *Guitar Book for Adult Beginners* includes free, bonus lessons. Go to the Home Page of SteeplechaseMusic.com. At the top of the Home Page, you will see a link for Guitar Books. Follow the link to the Guitar Books webpage. Then, click on the link for *Guitar Book for Adult Beginners*. Once you are on the webpage for the book, click Bonus Lessons and download the PDF file.

Table of Contents for the Video Lessons

Important!

To access the video lessons, go to steeplechasemusic.com and click on the link at the top of the page for Guitar Books. Then, from the Guitar Books webpage, click on the image for this book, "Guitar Book for Adult Beginners". On the webpage for the *Guitar Book for Adult Beginners*, you will see a link to Video Lessons. Click that link for the Video Lessons webpage for this book. The video lessons are free and there is no limit on the number of times you may watch them.

Steeplechase Music Books

Also by Damon Ferrante

Ultimate Guitar Chords, Scales & Arpeggios Handbook: 240-Lesson, Step-By-Step Guitar Guide, Beginner to Advanced Levels (Book & Videos)

Guitar Scales Handbook: A Step-By-Step, 100-Lesson Guide to Scales, Music Theory, and Fretboard Theory (Book & Videos)

Piano Scales, Chords & Arpeggios Lessons with Elements of Basic Music Theory: Fun, Step-By-Step Guide for Beginner to Advanced Levels (Book & Videos)

Little Piano Book for Children 5 & Up: Fun, Step-By-Step, Easy-To-Follow Beginner Piano Guide (Book & Videos)

Guitar: Book for Adult Beginners: Teach Yourself How to Play Famous Guitar Songs, Guitar Chords, Music Theory & Technique (Book & Streaming Video Lessons)

by Damon Ferrante

For additional information about
music books, recordings, and concerts,
please visit the Steeplechase website:
www.steeplechasemusic.com

Steeplechase Arts

ISBN-13:
978-0692996966 (Steeplechase Arts)

ISBN-10: 0692996966

Symbols used in this book

Left-Hand Symbols:

1 • **1st Finger (Index Finger)**

2 • **2nd Finger (Middle Finger)**

3 • **3rd Finger (Ring Finger)**

4 • **4th Finger (Pinky Finger)**

1 • **Place Finger over 2 or more strings.**

O • **Open String (Let the String Vibrate.)**

X • **Mute String (Block the String with a Finger.)**

Instructional Videos:

• There are 12 Supplemental Instructional Videos that correspond to the lessons presented in this Book.

• To access the videos, go to SteeplechaseMusic.com and click on the link for Guitar Books at top of the Home Page. Then, on the Guitar Books Page, click on the cover image for this book: *Guitar Book for Adult Beginners*. On the webpage for the book, you will see a link for the video lessons. Click on the link for access.

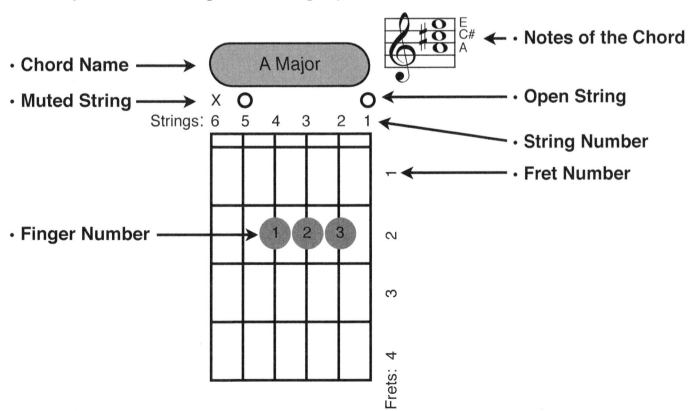

STARTING OUT

Types of Guitars

Parts of the Guitar

Names of the Strings

Basic Guitar Technique

Learning Songs

Strumming Techniques

Tuning The Guitar

Major Chords

Section Review

Lesson 1:
Secret to Guitar Success #1

Over the course of this book and videos, you will learn new techniques and licks, basic concepts about how music is put together (otherwise known as "music theory"), and songs. Interspersed alongside these music concepts are short essays entitled "Secrets to Guitar Success." The idea of these "secrets" is to give you a chance to step back from your playing and take a look at where you are and where you are going, musically speaking. The "secrets" are designed to be starting points for you to think about different aspects of your music making--from day-to-day matters to long-range plans. They are based on general concepts that I have learned over the years from teachers (both in music and other aspects of life) as well as insights from students. I hope that they might be ideas that you return to from time to time and that they help you in your progress to becoming a better musician.

Secret #1: *Have a Positive Attitude, Enjoy the Process, and Have Fun*

One of the most important aspects for learning an instrument is cultivating a positive attitude. If you approach learning guitar with a happy, fun-loving spirit your mind and body will be much more receptive to learning new ideas. Having a can-do, positive outlook will not only make the process of learning more fun, but it has been proven to speed up the process of improving. So, you should always approach your guitar playing as an exciting and rewarding activity of your day.

If you are feeling tired, a little down, or having a bad day and reluctant to practice your guitar, just remind yourself about how playing the guitar always makes you feel better and gives you positive energy. Sometimes, all it takes is grabbing your guitar, smiling and saying in your head -- "This is Fun!"

Give it a try!

Lesson 2: Types of Guitars

Acoustic Guitar   Solid-Body Electric Guitar   Hollow-Body Electric Guitar

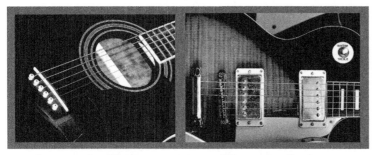

Acoustic Guitar Sound Hole   Electric Guitar Pickups

Although there are countless varieties of guitars in the world, ranging from neon-green, polka-dotted models to lightning-shaped ones, most guitars fit into three main, broad categories: Acoustic Guitars (Steel-String and Nylon-String), Solid-Body Electric Guitars, and Hollow-Body Electric Guitars.

Acoustic Guitars have a hollow body that allows for a natural amplification of the sound caused by the vibrating strings. Most Acoustic Guitars fall into two main categories: Steel-String and Nylon-String Guitars. Steel-String Guitars have all metal strings and, generally, have a bright and metallic sound. Nylon-String Guitars, often used for Classical guitar playing, have a combination of metal-wound strings for the low-sounding, bass strings and nylon strings for the thinner, higher-sounding strings.

Solid-Body Electric Guitars are the most common type of electric guitar. In and of themselves, they have a fairly quiet sound, since they do not have a hollow chamber (like acoustic guitars) to enhance the sound. For electric guitars, the sound of the vibrating strings is drawn from the wood of the guitar body through the pickups (a series of wound, magnetic coils) located below the strings in the center of the front of the guitar. (See Lesson 4 for more information). The sound then travels through a cable to an amplifier ("amp" for short).

Hollow-Body Electric Guitars are electric guitars that combine the features of Solid-Body Electric and Acoustic Guitars. They have a fairly resonant sound, in and of themselves, and they can also be amplified.

Lesson 3
Parts of an Acoustic Guitar

Here is an example of a steel-string acoustic guitar. They have a vibrant sound. In general, acoustic guitars have a higher action (the distance between the string and the fretboard). One of the benefits of acoustic guitars is that they are easily portable and don't need an amplifier.

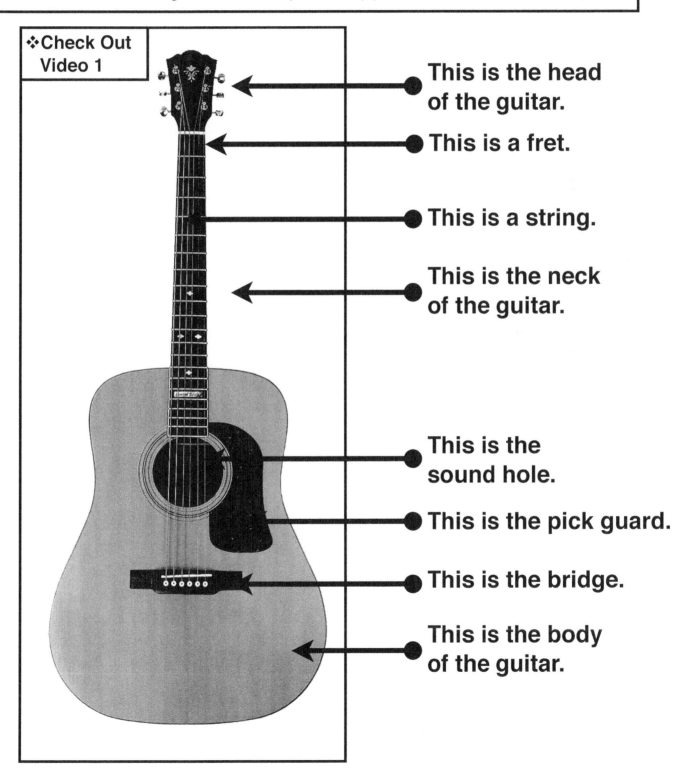

❖Check Out Video 1

This is the head of the guitar.

This is a fret.

This is a string.

This is the neck of the guitar.

This is the sound hole.

This is the pick guard.

This is the bridge.

This is the body of the guitar.

Lesson 4
Parts of an Electric Guitar

If you have an electric guitar, try to locate each of these parts. Since there is a wide range of design styles for electric guitars, you will probably find a few differences (in some of the details) from the electric guitar example in the illustration below.

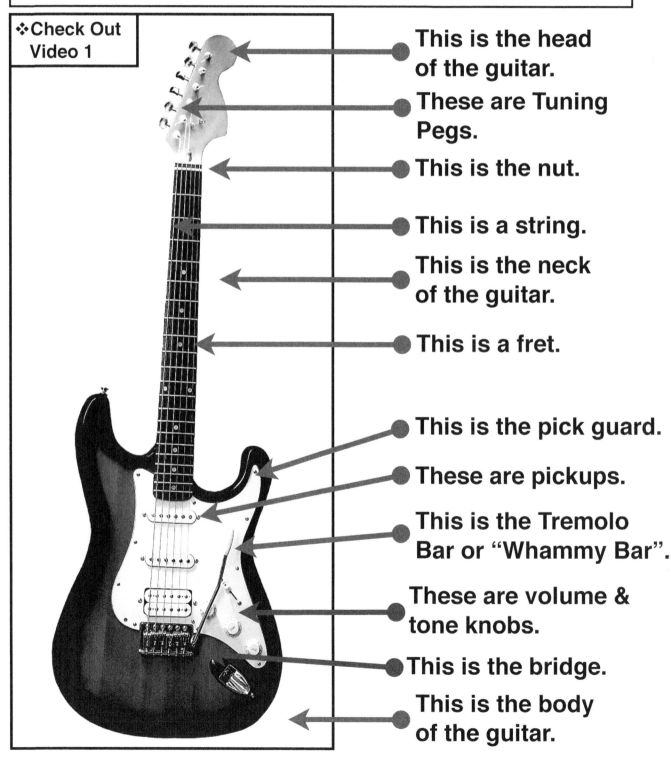

❖Check Out Video 1

This is the head of the guitar.

These are Tuning Pegs.

This is the nut.

This is a string.

This is the neck of the guitar.

This is a fret.

This is the pick guard.

These are pickups.

This is the Tremolo Bar or "Whammy Bar".

These are volume & tone knobs.

This is the bridge.

This is the body of the guitar.

Lesson 5: An Explanation of the Different Parts of the Guitar

The **Head** of the guitar is the top section of the guitar. It holds the tuning pegs. There is often a company logo on the head of the guitar.

The **Tuning Pegs** (sometimes called "machine heads") are metal or plastic knobs, located on the guitar head. They allow the guitarist to adjust the tension on the strings. By turning a tuning peg and increasing the tension on the string, the sound of that string will have a higher pitch. The opposite is true if you loosen the tension on the string: the sound of the string will be lower.

The **Neck** of the guitar is a long section of wood that connects the head and body of the guitar. The frets and fingerboard are on the top of the neck.

The **Nut** is a small piece of plastic or wood, located between the head and neck. The nut helps keep the strings above the frets and fingerboard.

The **Frets** are rectangular boxes that run up and down the guitar neck. They are created by small strips of metal that cover the guitar neck at precise spacing. These frets create the specific notes on the guitar, for instance, the note "C" or the note "F-Sharp". At the head of the guitar, the frets are wider. As you travel "up" the guitar neck toward the body, the frets become thinner, because the pitches ("sounds") are getting higher.

The **Body** of the guitar is a large, often curved, section of wood. On acoustic guitars it holds the bridge, sound hole, and pick guard. On electric guitars, it is the part of the guitar that holds the pickups, bridge, tone and volume knobs, toggle switch, pick guard, and whammy bar.

The **Pickups** are sets of wound, magnetic coils. They are often housed in plastic or metal casings. The pickups draw the vibrations from the strings and send them through the cable to the amplifier. (We will go into more detail about pickups and amplifiers later in this book. They are an important part of the character of each electric guitar's sound.)

The **Bridge** is a piece of wood or metal that is located on the body of the guitar. The strings are held in tension between the bridge and the tuning pegs of the guitar.

The **Sound Hole** is the circular hole on the body of an acoustic guitar. The sound of the vibrating strings travels through the sound hole in the the body of an acoustic guitar. The sound is then "amplified" by the interior of the guitar body and projected back out of the sound hole.

The **Tremolo Bar** (or "Whammy Bar") is a metal bar attached to the bridge of electric guitars. It allows the guitarist to pull up or push down on the bridge and increase or decrease the tension on the strings: raising or lowing the sound of the notes.

The **Volume** and **Tone** knobs on an electric guitar raise and lower the loudness of the guitar's sound and also change the balance of treble and bass sound for the guitar. On an electric guitar, these knobs can greatly change the sound of the instrument. In some ways these knobs create "many instruments in one".

Lesson 6: Names of the Guitar Strings & Finger Numbers

In this lesson, we are going to learn two concepts:
The letter names for the guitar strings and the finger numbers for the left hand.

Low   **High**
E   A   D   G   B   E

The Guitar Strings

- 6th String, **Low E** = **Ernie**
- 5th String, **A** = **Always**
- 4th String, **D** = **Drinks**
- 3rd String, **G** = **Grape Juice**
- 2nd String, **B** = **Before**
- 1st String, **High E** = **Eating**

- The guitar has six strings.
- The strings have numbers that go from the thinnest string to the thickest string.
- The thinnest string is string #1. It is located closest to the floor and it has the highest sound.
- The thickest string is string #6. It is located closest to the ceiling and has the lowest (or deepest) sound.
- The thinnest string (the first string) is called the "High-E String".
- The thickest string (the sixth string) is called the "Low-E String".
- Going from thickest string to thinnest string, here are the letter names for the strings:

Low E, A, D, G, B, High E

- To help you remember the letter names and order for the strings, here is a silly sentence: **E**rnie **A**lways **D**rinks **G**rape Juice **B**efore **E**ating.
- The first letter of each word (**except for "juice"**) stands for a string of the guitar, going from thickest string to thinnest string. **See the chart on the left.**

- Try this exercise: While holding your guitar, try to find the Low-E String and play it. Now, try to find the High-E String and play it.
- Now, go through all of the strings, from Low E to High E, and play them in order (thickest string to thinnest), while saying the letter name for each string.

Left-Hand Finger Numbers:
Index Finger = 1, Middle Finger = 2, Ring Finger = 3, Pinky = 4

Lesson 7: Holding the Pick & Left-Hand Technique

Holding the guitar pick

Try this exercise: Find the 1st string (the High-E String). With a downward motion, pluck the string 10 times in a row. Then, with an upward motion, pluck the string 10 times in a row. Repeat this.

Let's look at how to hold the guitar pick.

- Gently place the guitar pick on the finger nail of your Right-Hand Index Finger.

- It should be resting gently on top of your finger nail.

- Then, slide it to the left side of your Index Finger.

- Finally, gently place your Right-Hand Thumb over over the guitar pick. It should be held between your Right-Hand Thumb and Index Finger. (See the Photo on the left.)

Left-Hand Technique

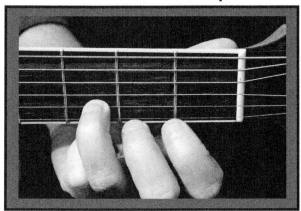

Try this exercise (see the photo above): Place the 3rd finger of your left hand on the 3rd fret of the 2nd string (the B String). Pluck the string with your pick. This is the note "D", by the way. Then, lift your finger off the string and pluck the open string. This is the note "B". Repeat this 10 times in a row.

Let's Look at Basic Left-Hand Technique

- For most of your guitar playing you are going to want to play the guitar notes with the tips of your left-hand fingers. (By the way, this is called "fretting" the notes.) This technique will create the best guitar tone and diminish any string buzzing.

- For the majority of your fretted notes, you should bring your left-hand thumb down so that it roughly lines up, on the back side of the guitar neck with your index finger.

- For some fretted notes, you will need to use a moderate amount of hand strength to make the notes sound.

Lesson 8: Secret to Guitar Success #2 Developing Good Practice Habits

One of the most important aspects of playing the guitar is forming good practice habits. Learning the guitar is a fun and creative endeavor; if you develop good practice habits you will make rapid progress with your playing. This will require a little bit of focus and a proactive attitude on your part. However, it will make a big difference for you.

Ideally, you should strive to practice around five to seven times per week (once per day) for about 20 to 40 minutes. If you have more time, that's great. However, it's best to spend your time practicing well (in an organized manner), rather than just spending a lot of time practicing. Along these lines, one of the most important facets of learning to play the guitar is having some continuity in your practice routine. So, even on days that you are extremely busy, try to take 10-15 minutes to work on your guitar playing. As best as you can, try to avoid missing more than three days of practicing in a row.

For the most positive results, you should strive to be organized with your practicing: have a plan for each practice session and have a few weekly goals. For example, a plan for a practice session might include spending 10 minutes on a technique or warm-up exercises, working on a lesson or two from this book for 20 minutes, and practicing a song for 15 minutes. Some examples for weekly goals might include working on four to five lessons from this book, practicing a song that you like, and spending 10 minutes a day on technique-improving exercises for your guitar playing. It should also be said that your weekly goals should not be too rigid (for example, "I *must* learn all of *Layla* this week.") or extremely lofty (for example, "This week, I'm going to learn 20 Foo Fighters' songs.").

Although letting your unconscious mind roam freely as you strum the guitar and noodle around with riffs and licks on the instrument is one important element to learning, discovery and improvement in music, try to keep this aspect of your playing to about 25% of your practicing. Sadly, many guitarists spend way too much time noodling around with their favorite sections of songs, ones that they are very comfortable playing. This often leads to guitarists falling into ruts with their playing (staying at the same level without improving). Though it is a lot of fun to noodle around on the guitar and play little riffs and licks, it's very important to be focused about your practicing and set clear goals for about 75% of your work time.

So, let's get started: Your lesson for today is to find a notebook or looseleaf binder that will be your practice journal. It does not have to be anything fancy or expensive. Take a few moments now to find one. If you do not have one around the house, buy one for a few dollars at a local store or online. This little investment will yield very positive results. Now, on the first page of the journal, write today's date, a lesson or two from this book that you would like to work on, and how much time you plan on spending on your guitar practice. You should continue this process for each day you practice. Some people like to cross off each task as they complete it. As well, it's often a good idea to write your next day's practice schedule at the end of your current day's practice session. This way, at some level, your mind will already be thinking about and planning for the next day's work; it's a good way to build and sustain momentum.

Lesson 9: Right-Hand Strumming Exercises & Counting Beats

Strumming the Guitar and Counting Beats: In this lesson we are going to work on right-hand strumming technique and also start learning how to count beats. Beats are the pulses in music that give it a clear rhythm. Most guitar music is based on groups of four beats. So, we count "One, Two, Three, Four". Each number equals one beat. Try this exercise, when you are listening to some music (in the car, on your way to school or work, at home, etc.): Try to find the beats of the song that you are listening to by counting "One, Two, Three, Four" in your mind. Quite often in Rock and Pop music, there is an accent (a stronger pulse) on the first beat ("Beat One") of each group of four beats. Locating this strong first beat with your ear will help you.

Exercise 1: With the pick in your right hand strum down on the High-E string four times in a row. The High-E string is the thinnest string on your guitar. It is called the "High-E string" because it has the highest pitch ("sound"). Try this exercise 10 times in a row. Count out loud one beat for each down strum, like this: "One, Two, Three, Four".

(Count Beat One louder, since it is the strongest beat of the four.)

Down-Strum Pattern:

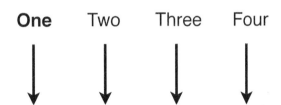

One   Two   Three   Four

Exercise 2: With the pick in your right hand strum down on the both High-E string and the B string (the second string) together four times in a row. Use a gentle, downward motion, like you are petting a cat. Repeat this exercise 10 times in a row. Count "One, Two, Three, Four" for each down strum / beat. Try slightly varying the strength of your down strums. As you do this, listen to the change in the sound quality.

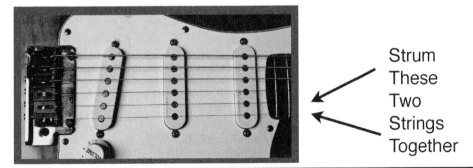

Strum These Two Strings Together

Exercise 3: Now, with the pick in your right hand strum down on the High-E string, the B string (the second string), and the G string (the third string) together four times in a row. Use a gentle, downward motion, like you are petting a cat. Repeat this exercise 10 times in a row. Count "One, Two, Three, Four" for each down strum / beat. Try slightly varying the strength of your down strums. As you do this, listen to the change in the sound quality.

Lesson 10: Easy Major Chords
C Major, F Major and G Major

In this lesson, we are going to learn three new chords (in easy-to-play format): C Major, F Major and G Major (see the diagrams).

For C Major, place your Index Finger on the First Fret of the Second String (the B String) and play Strings 1, 2 and 3 together.

For F Major, place your Index Finger on the First Fret of the Second String (the B String) and place your Middle Finger on the First Fret of the First String (the High-E String), and your Ring Finger on the Second Fret of the Third String (the G String). Play Strings 1, 2, and 3 together.

For G Major, place your Ring Finger on the Third Fret of the First String (the E String) and play Strings 1, 2, and 3 together.

Remember to place the tips of your left-hand fingers on the strings when you play chords.

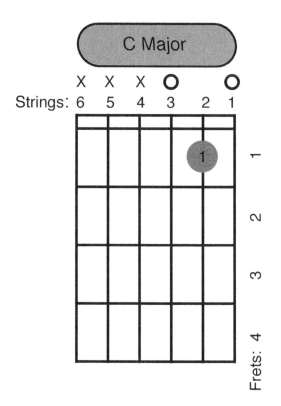

Please Note: The "X" symbol above the strings in these diagrams means don't play those strings. The "O" above the strings means play the string "open" (without any left-hand fingers).

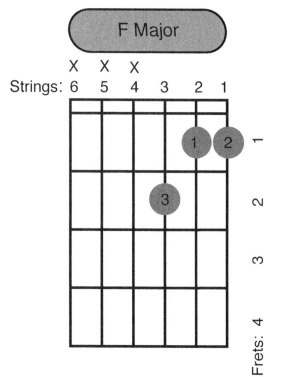

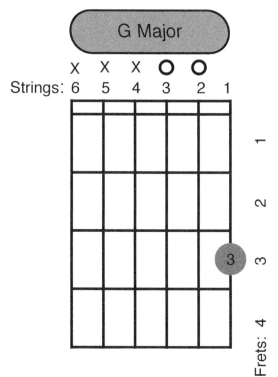

Lesson 11: Strumming Basics & *Three Chords and the Truth*

❖ Check
Out
Video 2

In the previous lesson, you have had a chance to practice these three basic chord forms: C Major, F Major, and G Major. Now, let's put them into action in a song. In *Three Chords and the Truth*, there are three lines of music. A line of music can also be called a "system" (in musical terminology).

Each system in this song has four measures. Measures are groups of beats. Most Rock and Pop songs are grouped into measures that have four beats. In music terminology these four-beat measure groups are called "4/4 time". We'll go into more detail about this later, but for now, let's just count "1, 2, 3, 4" for each measure of *Three Chords and the Truth*.

For each measure of *Three Chords and the Truth,* play four down strums on the chord and count (aloud or in your mind "1, 2, 3, 4"). For example, for the first measure, play four down strums on the C chord and count one beat (aloud or in your mind) for each down strum.

Before playing the entire song, try switching between four down strums on the C chord and then four down strums on the F chord. After you are comfortable with alternating between these two chords, try switching between four down strums on the C chord and then four down strums on the G chord

Three Chords and the Truth

C		C		F		F
C		C		G		G
F		F		C		C

Lesson 12: Strumming and Chord Changes, Part 2

Let's now continue working on a tune that uses the three major chords that we learned from the previous lesson: C Major, G Major, and F Major

For each measure of this song try to do this strumming pattern: Down Strum on the 1st Beat, Up Strum on the 2nd Beat, Down Strum on the 3rd Beat, Up Strum on the 4th Beat. Check out the diagram.

Practice each measure slowly and put one line (or system) together at a time.

Have Fun!

Down-Strum / Up-Strum Pattern:

One	Two	Three	Four
↓	↑	↓	↑

Tones

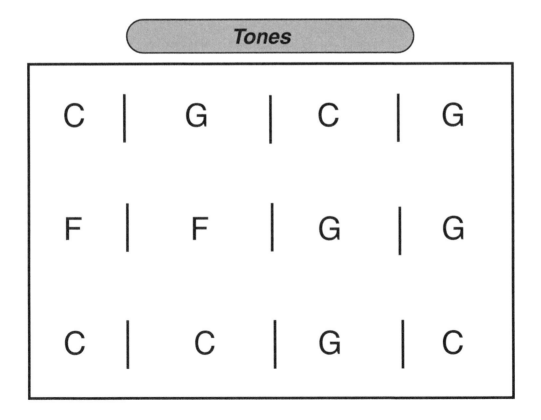

C	G	C	G
F	F	G	G
C	C	G	C

Lesson 13: Secret to Guitar Success #3 Patience & Longterm Perspective

Have patience and a longterm perspective: You are embarking on a grand and lifelong adventure in music. Through this journey, you will discover new perspectives on sound, communication, friendship, success, coordination, self confidence, concentration, memory, and determination. For the most part, this learning will be a step-by-step process, where your ability and understanding of music will move ahead at a gradual pace. At other times, your progress may suddenly leap ahead to another level in a flash of inspiration.

Whatever your goals in music may be, it's best to cultivate an attitude that music is a lifelong journey and process of creating and developing. As an artist, you should continue to explore and develop your musical voice. Life will take you along different paths and these will be reflected in your music making. Enjoy this adventure, especially if you are just beginning. You are like some explorer stepping onto the deck of your ship heading out from your land's port to find yet-unexplored, new places. Enjoy the journey!

In the next three lessons, we are going to look at three different methods for tuning your guitar. Each has its own benefit. So, you should spend time with all three methods to develop your skills. It may take a little while to cultivate your musical ear to hear the sometimes fine distinction between notes and strings that are in tune and ones that are a little bit out of tune. Just be patient with this skill. Over time and with practice you will be creating a very solid foundation for your musical hearing and understanding.

Playing in tune is a very important aspect of music and will make a huge difference in your sound, the development of your musical ear, and the respect that you will garner from fellow musicians and audience members. For most people, listening to someone play or sing out of tune elicits emotions ranging from annoyance to hilarity. If you have ever heard a violin concert performed by elementary students playing out of tune on screechy violins, you know what I mean. Although there is something charming about youngsters playing, you might not want to play a recording of the performance on your car stereo afterward.

So, the bottom line here is tuning is very important.

Lesson 14
Tuning the Guitar, Part 1

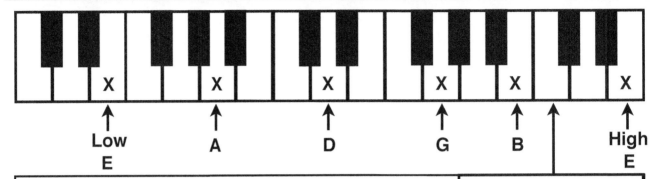

Low E   A   D   G   B   High E

**Middle C
(for the piano)**

For this first method of tuning the guitar, you will need to have access to a piano, keyboard, or music app (like Garage Band, Logic, etc.) that has a mini piano keyboard feature. There are also a number of websites that have good, free virtual piano keyboards. You might try typing "piano keyboard" or "virtual piano keyboard" into a search engine like Google. A number of possible choices should show up in the search results.

In the chart above of the piano keyboard locate the piano key with the "X" that is labeled "Low E". Now on the piano, keyboard, or virtual "app" piano locate the key for "Low E" and play it. It should be located in the left-region of the piano keyboard. After you play the note on your keyboard, pluck the Low-E (the thickest) string of your guitar and listen to the sound. Try to match the sound of the keyboard, "Low-E note" by turning the tuning peg of your guitar either clockwise or counterclockwise.

As you get close to matching the pitch (sound) of the piano with your guitar, you will hear a kind of wavy / warbling sound as the guitar note aligns with the piano note. When the warbling / quavering stops and the notes are the same, you will be in unison ("in tune") with the piano note.

Now, locate the key in the piano chart above that is marked "A". Once you have done this, find and play the corresponding key for "A" on your piano keyboard (whether real or virtual). While the piano note for "A" is sounding pluck the 5th string of your guitar. This is the A string. Turn the tuning peg for the A string and match the pitch on your guitar with the pitch of the piano sound. Just as with the Low-E string, as you get closer to matching the "A" pitch in the piano with you guitar, you will hear a quavering in the pitch that goes from slow to fast as you tune in closer. Once the warbling stops and you have matched the "A" piano pitch, your "A" string will be in tune.

Repeat this same process of finding the note on your keyboard, playing it, and then matching it on your guitar for the next four strings: the D, G, B and High E (in order from thickest to thinnest). The notes / keys on your keyboard for this tuning method will go from left to right. Left is for the lower (deeper-sounding) notes on the piano. Right is for the higher sounds notes. This corresponds to the guitar strings going from thicker strings (with deeper sounds, like the Low-E string) to thinner strings (like the High E).

Lesson 15
Tuning the Guitar, Part 2

❖**Check
Out
Video 3**

This next method for tuning can be used in conjunction with a tuning fork, pitch pipe, fixed-pitch instrument (like a piano, keyboard, harmonica, etc., if one is available), or just the guitar itself, if it is relatively in tune.

First, a little bit of background information: When the guitar is in standard tuning (that is, Low E, A, D, G, B, High E), a note on an adjacent thicker string fretted on the fifth fret (or in one case, the fourth fret) will match the note of its adjacent thinner open string in unison. In other words, when you place your finger on the 5th fret of the Low-E string (the 6th string), you will play the note "A". This is the same note as the open 5th String: the A string.

Give it a try. Put a finger on the 5th fret of the Low-E string and pluck the string. Now, play the 5th string (the A string) open (with no fingers pressing on a fret). It should be the same sound. If not, adjust the tuning peg for the A string to match the pitch of the fretted "A" note on the Low-E string (**see the video lesson on tuning for a demonstration**). Follow the same process for the A string and D string, as well as the D string and G string. (See chart below.) To tune the B string, play the note of the 4th fret of the G string (3rd string). This is the note "B", and then play the open B string. To tune the High-E string, play the 5th fret of the B string.

● Place your index finger down on the location of the black dot in the places indicated in the diagram below.

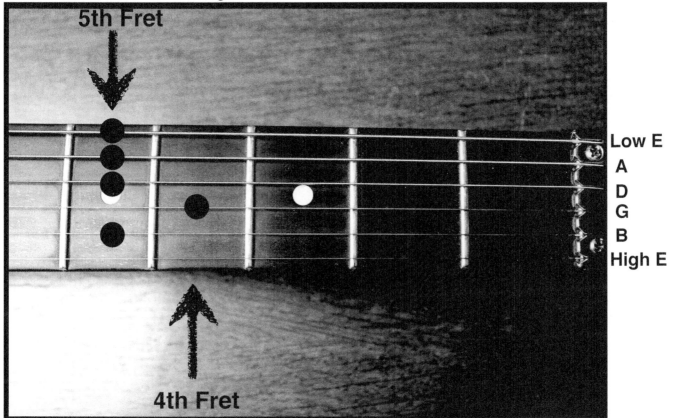

Lesson 16: Tuning the Guitar, Part 3 Portable, Electronic Guitar Tuners

Types of portable, electronic guitar tuners:
1. Clip-On Tuner 2. Smartphone App 3. Tablet App

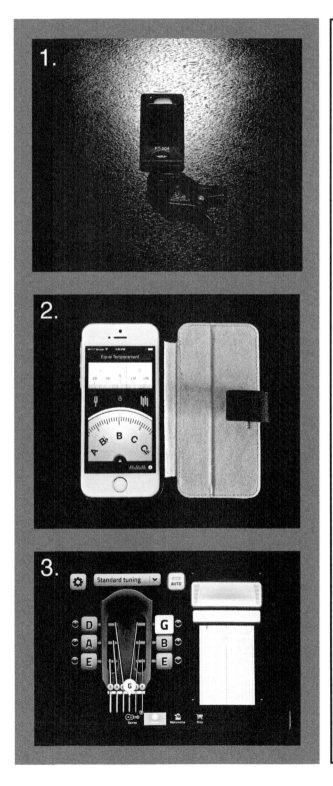

Electronic Tuners

Along with tuning the guitar by the methods previously detailed the last two lessons, it is also a good idea to get a portable electronic tuner. This is not a big rush; however, you might like to have one sometime over the next year or two, as you start playing music with family and friends, and also start to perform around your town and area.

There are several benefits to having a portable tuner. First off, you can tune the guitar quickly with a great deal of accuracy. You can also check your guitar's tuning after playing a few songs (during a practice session, band rehearsal, or performance). Next, you can tune the guitar accurately without access to a piano, keyboard, pitch pipe, tuning fork, or fixed-pitch tuning instrument or device.

These tuners come in all sorts of shapes and sizes. The most popular and practical are clip-on tuners (in the illustration at the top to the left) and guitar-tuner apps (in the middle and bottom illustrations to the left). They range in prices from free (for many of the Apps that will work on smartphones, tablets, and computers) to around twenty dollars. You can find them online or at your local music store.

Lesson 17
Major Chords: Open Position

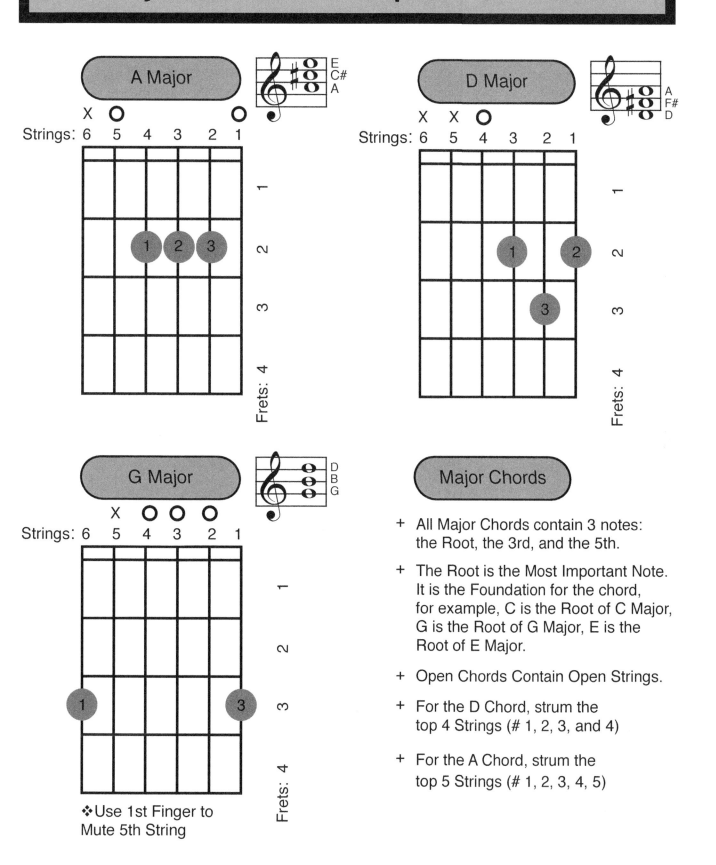

A Major

Strings: 6 5 4 3 2 1

E C# A

Frets: 1 2 3 4

D Major

Strings: 6 5 4 3 2 1

A F# D

Frets: 1 2 3 4

G Major

Strings: 6 5 4 3 2 1

D B G

Frets: 1 2 3 4

❖ Use 1st Finger to Mute 5th String

Major Chords

+ All Major Chords contain 3 notes: the Root, the 3rd, and the 5th.

+ The Root is the Most Important Note. It is the Foundation for the chord, for example, C is the Root of C Major, G is the Root of G Major, E is the Root of E Major.

+ Open Chords Contain Open Strings.

+ For the D Chord, strum the top 4 Strings (# 1, 2, 3, and 4)

+ For the A Chord, strum the top 5 Strings (# 1, 2, 3, 4, 5)

Lesson 18
Amazing Grace

Measure Line

Chord:	D	D	G	D
	A-mazing	Grace how	sweet the	sound that
Strum:	1 2 3	1 2 3	1 2 3	1 2 3

Chord:	D	D	A	A
	saved a	wretch like	me.	I
Strum:	1 2 3	1 2 3	1 2 3	1 2 3

Chord:	D	D	G	D
	once was	lost but	now am	found. Was
Strum:	1 2 3	1 2 3	1 2 3	1 2 3

Chord:	D	A	D	D
	blind but	now I	see.	
Strum:	1 2 3	1 2 3	1 2 3	1 2 3

Measures

+ Music is composed of groups of beats called measures.

+ Measures are set off by two vertical lines.

+ Measures most commonly contain 2, 3, or 4 beats.

+ Our first song, Amazing Grace, has 3 beats in each measure.

+ Strum the chords of Amazing Grace 3 times for each measure.

+ Start strumming on the second syllable of the word "Amazing".

Amazing Grace

+ Amazing Grace uses the D, G, and A major chords.

+ The chords are shown above the words.

+ The beats (or strum patterns) are shown below the words.

+ Practice each line slowly, while singing the words aloud or in your head.

+ Try forming a chord once and strum. Then, place your left hand on your lap and repeat the process for each chord 10-20 times.

Lesson 19: Counting & Measures

- Below, are examples of sets of four measures in 4/4 time.
- In 4/4 time, you will count 4 beats for each measure.
  In other words, you will count: 1234, 1234, 1234, 1234.
- Try counting aloud and clapping the beats for the exercise below.

Example 1:

| 1 2 3 4 | 1 2 3 4 | 1 2 3 4 | 1 2 3 4 ||

Example 2:
Try Clapping on the X: On the First Beat.

| 1 2 3 4 | 1 2 3 4 | 1 2 3 4 | 1 2 3 4 ||
| X | X | X | X |

Example 3:
Try Clapping on the X: On the First and Third Beats.

| 1 2 3 4 | 1 2 3 4 | 1 2 3 4 | 1 2 3 4 ||
| X   X | X   X | X   X | X   X |

Example 4:
Try Clapping on the X: On the Second Beat.

| 1 2 3 4 | 1 2 3 4 | 1 2 3 4 | 1 2 3 4 ||
| X | X | X | X |

Lesson 20
Major Chords: Open Position

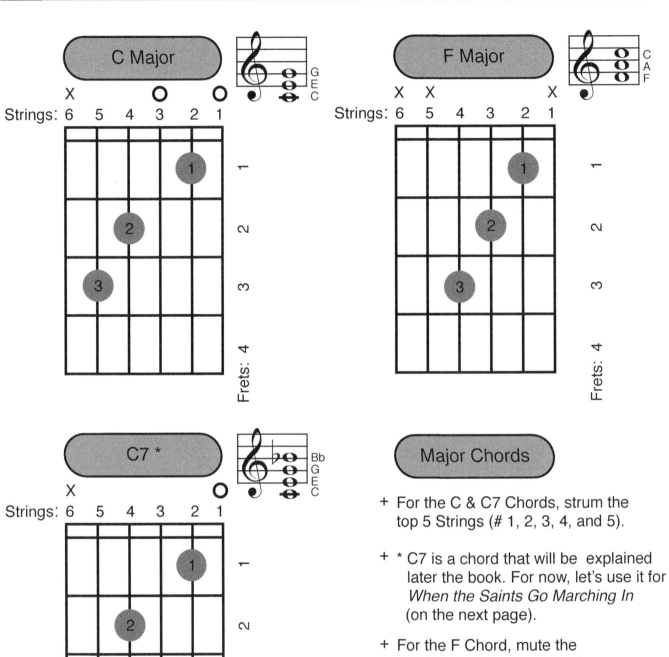

C Major

Strings: 6 5 4 3 2 1

GEC

F Major

Strings: 6 5 4 3 2 1

CAF

C7 *

Strings: 6 5 4 3 2 1

Bb
G
E
C

Major Chords

+ For the C & C7 Chords, strum the top 5 Strings (# 1, 2, 3, 4, and 5).

+ * C7 is a chord that will be explained later the book. For now, let's use it for *When the Saints Go Marching In* (on the next page).

+ For the F Chord, mute the 1st String with your index finger (and strum the top 4 Strings (# 1, 2, 3, and 4)

+ To help improve your speed in changing from one chord to the next, try placing one finger down at a time. It is best to place the 1st, then 2nd, and 3rd fingers (index, middle, and ring fingers) in succession.

Lesson 21
When the Saints Go Marching In

Chord:	(No Chord)	C	C	C
	Oh When the	Saints	go marchin' in	in
Strum:	1 2 3 4	1 2 3 4	1 2 3 4	1 2 3 4
Chord: C		C	C7	G
	Oh When the	Saints go	marchin'	in
Strum:	1 2 3 4	1 2 3 4	1 2 3 4	1 2 3 4
Chord: G		C	C7	F
	Oh Lord, I	want to	be in that	number
Strum:	1 2 3 4	1 2 3 4	1 2 3 4	1 2 3 4
Chord: F		C	G	C
	Oh When the	Saints go	marchin'	in
Strum:	1 2 3 4	1 2 3 4	1 2 3 4	1 2 3 4

Upbeats

+ In music, there are many songs and pieces that use upbeats.

+ An upbeat (or upbeats) are notes that occur before the first full measure of a song.

+ Upbeats act as a very short introductory phrases that emphasize an important note or word at the beginning of a song. For example, in *When the Saints Go Marchin' In,* the words "Oh when the" are the upbeat. They lead into and accentuate the word "saints".

When the *Saints*

+ *When the Saints uses* the C, F, and G major chords.

+ The chords are shown above the words.

+ The beats (or strum patterns) are show below the words.

+ Practice each line slowly, while singing the words aloud or in your head.

+ If you cannot remember one of the chords, review the chord diagrams on the previous pages.

+ Strum the Chords 4 times for each measure.

Lesson 22
1st & 2nd String Notes

In this lesson, we are going to look at six notes on the first and second strings (the high-E string and the B string). We will be playing these notes in future songs; so, take some time now to commit them to memory.

Looking at the chart below, locate the following notes on your guitar: B, D, E, G, C, and F.

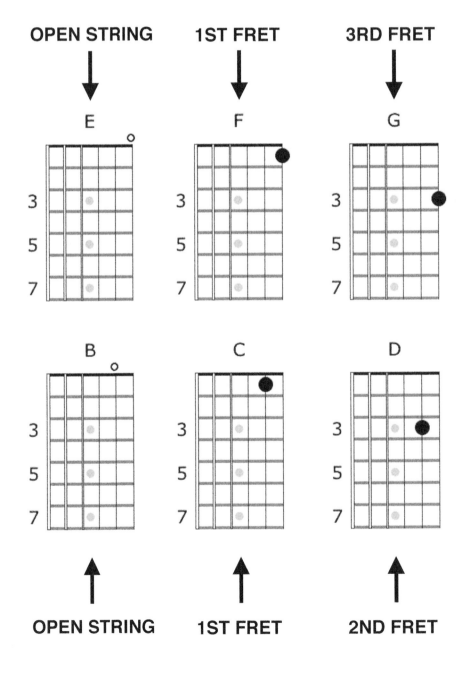

Lesson 23
Ode to Joy & Jingle Bells

Let's now check out these two classics: *Ode to Joy* (by Beethoven) and *Jingle Bells.* The melodies for both of these songs are located on the first and second strings of the guitar (High-E and B strings).

The numbers here are for <u>beats</u>, not fingers. When there is a blank space, don't play for that beat or beats.

Ode to Joy

Beats:	1	2	3	4		1	2	3	4		1	2	3	4		1	2	3	4	
	E	E	F	G		G	F	E	D		C	C	D	E		E	D	D		

FIRST STRING   SECOND STRING

Beats:	1	2	3	4		1	2	3	4		1	2	3	4		1	2	3	4	
	E	E	F	G		G	F	E	D		C	C	D	E		D	C	C		

Jingle Bells

Beats:	1	2	3	4		1	2	3	4		1	2	3	4		1	2	3	4	
	E	E	E			E	E	E			E	G	C	D		E				
	Jin-	gle	Bells,			Jin-	gle	Bells,			Jin-	gle	all	the		way.				

FIRST STRING   SECOND STRING

Beats:	1	2	3	4		1	2	3	4		1	2	3	4		1	2	3	4	
	F	F	F	F		F	E	E	E		E	D	D	E		D		G		
	Oh!	What	fun	it		is	to	ride	in		a	one-horse	open	sleigh!		Hey!				

Lesson 24
3rd & 4th String Notes

In this lesson, we are going to look at six notes on the third and fourth strings (the G and the D strings). We will be playing these notes in future songs; so, take some time now to commit them to memory.

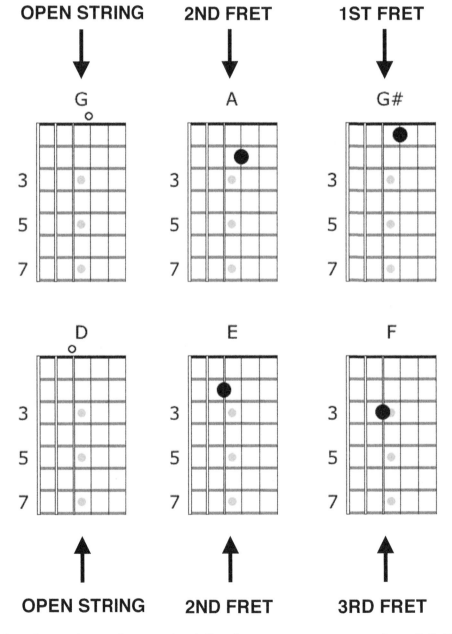

Looking at the chart above, locate the following notes on your guitar: G#, D, E, G, A, and F.

Lesson 25: Upbeats & *When the Saints Go Marching In*

- In music, there are many songs and pieces that use Upbeats.
- An Upbeat (or Upbeats) are a note or group of notes that occur before the first full measure of a song or piece of music.
- Upbeats act as very short introductory phrases that emphasize an important note or word at the beginning of a song. For example, in *When the Saints Go Marching In,* the words "Oh when the" are the upbeat. They lead into and accentuate the word "saints".

These Upbeats Start on Beat 2

Do you notice how both of these phases -- "Oh, When the Saints" and "Go Marching In"-- start on the 2nd Beat? These are Upbeat figures.

$\frac{4}{4}$

1 2 3 4	1 2 3 4	1 2 3 4	1 2 3 4
Oh, When the	Saints	go March-ing	in.

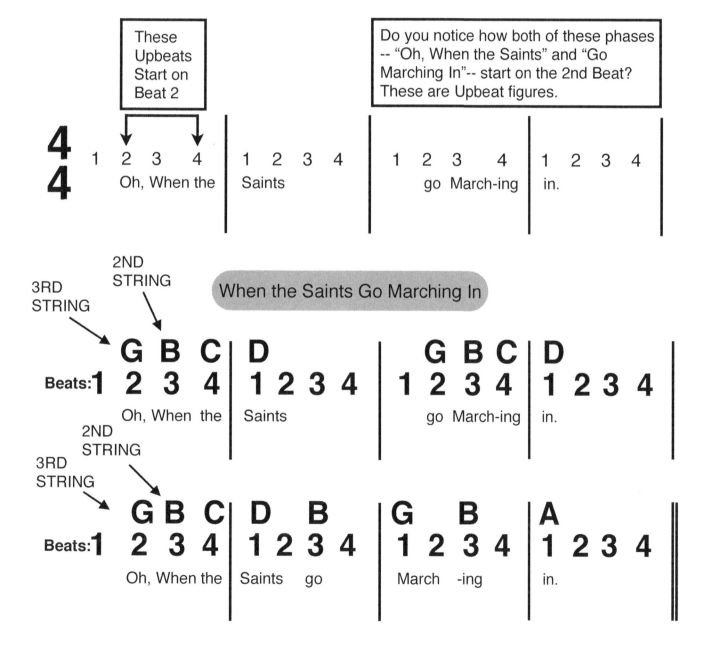

3RD STRING
2ND STRING

When the Saints Go Marching In

G B C | D
Beats:1 2 3 4 | 1 2 3 4

G B C | D
1 2 3 4 | 1 2 3 4

Oh, When the | Saints

go March-ing | in.

2ND STRING
3RD STRING

G B C| D B | G B | A
Beats:1 2 3 4 | 1 2 3 4 | 1 2 3 4 | 1 2 3 4

Oh, When the | Saints go | March -ing | in.

Lesson 26
5th & 6th String Notes

In this lesson, we are going to look at six notes on the fifth and sixth strings (the A and the Low-E strings). We will be playing these notes in future songs; so, take some time now to commit them to memory.

OPEN STRING   **2ND FRET**   **3RD FRET**

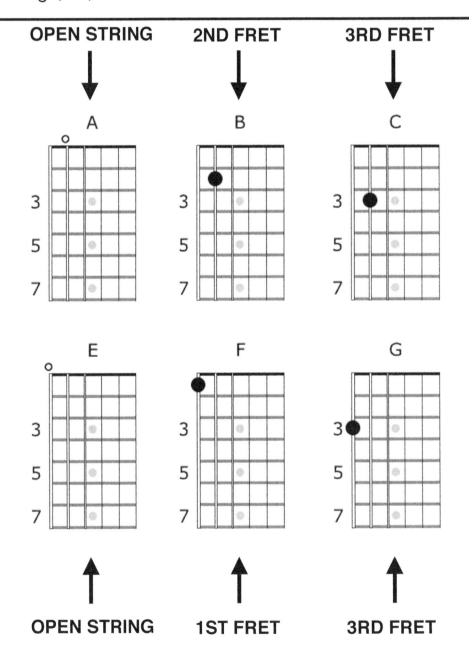

OPEN STRING   **1ST FRET**   **3RD FRET**

Looking at the chart above, locate the following notes on your guitar: B, C, E, G, A, and F.

Lesson 27: Whole Notes, Half Notes & Quarter Notes

- Let's take a look at some basic rhythms.
- Quarter Notes are notes that get 1 Beat (or Count).
- Half Notes are notes that get 2 Beats (or Counts).
- Whole Notes are notes that get 4 Beats (or Counts).
- In the next 3 examples, try counting on each beat of the 4/4 measures aloud, for example: 1,2,3,4.
- Clap on the quarter, half, and whole notes.

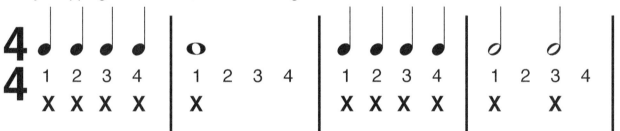

♩ = 1 Beat   ♩ = 2 Beats   o = 4 Beats

Example 1:
Try Clapping on each "X", while counting the beats.

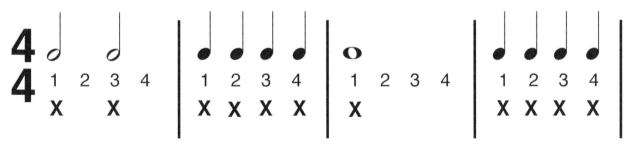

Example 2:
Try Clapping on each "X", while counting the beats.

Example 3:
Try Clapping on each "X", while counting the beats.

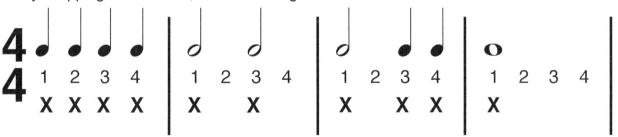

Lesson 28: Tablature Basics

Guitar tablature (or TAB for short) is a notation system that graphically indicates guitar fingering, rather than the actual notes and pitches to be played. In other words, TAB shows you the exact location on strings and frets where you will need to play, but it does not tell you the actual notes (for example, "Eb", G, B) or the rhythms and durations of what you will be playing. Tablature is a good initial "shorthand" notation, especially if you are already familiar with a song, but it might have some drawbacks if you solely rely on it to learn music. For this book, we will use tablature and video examples. Later on in your playing, you might like to start learning standard notation, which will give you a more accurate representation of what's going on in music than tablature.

Here is how TAB works: The thickest string (Low-E string) is the bottom line of the tablature staff and the thinnest string (High-E string) is the top line of the tablature staff. So, the higher lines on the staff represent the higher-pitched guitar strings and the lower lines on the tablature staff represent the lower-pitched guitar strings. A note on the guitar is indicated by placing a number on one of the lines of the tablature staff. The number represents which fret to place your finger on and the line indicates which string to play. However, tablature does not indicate how long to play the note, which left-hand finger to use, or how loud to play the note. As mentioned above, it does not indicate the actual name of the note ("pitch") that you are playing. It does, though, sometimes indicate other qualities of the note--for example, if you are supposed to bend the note, play a pull off or hammer on, or give vibrato (more about all of these techniques later on in the book).

Chords are represented by placing the numbers on top of each other on the TAB staff. The number zero indicates that you should play an open string.

One last thing, even though tablature has been around for centuries (it was used frequently in the Renaissance), there is not a one-hundred-percent set system for the notation. So, you might see slight variations among the TAB versions in a number of Rock, Pop, Country, Folk, and Gospel songbooks or online TAB-versions of songs.

Tablature Example of the C Major Chord from Lesson 10
(See the Chord chart on Lesson 10)

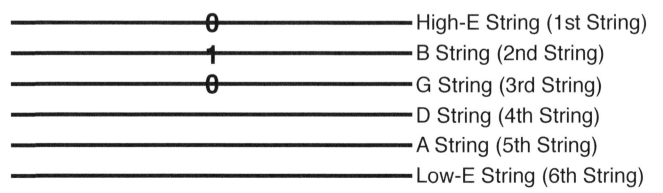

Lesson 29
The Melody for *Amazing Grace*

In this lesson, we are going to look at the melody for *Amazing Grace.* This version of the song is in the key of G, which allows us to play the many of the melody notes on open strings. The melody for this lesson's version is in a different key from the version we learned earlier in the book.

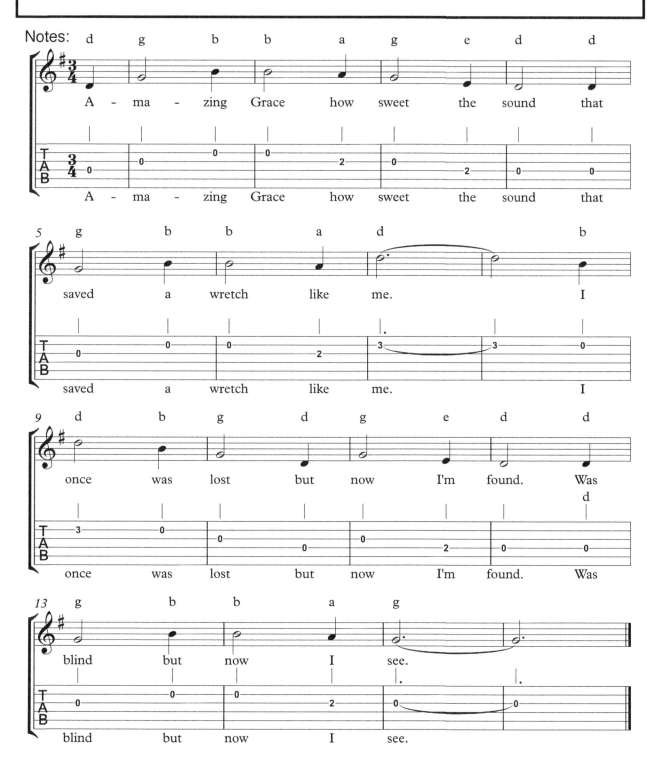

Lesson 30: The Melody for
When the Saints Go Marching In

Now let's take a look at the melody for *When the Saints Go Marching In*. Remember, when you are playing this piece, to anticipate the upbeat figures that start each musical phrase. You might want to check back on the earlier lessons that explain upbeats, if you have questions.

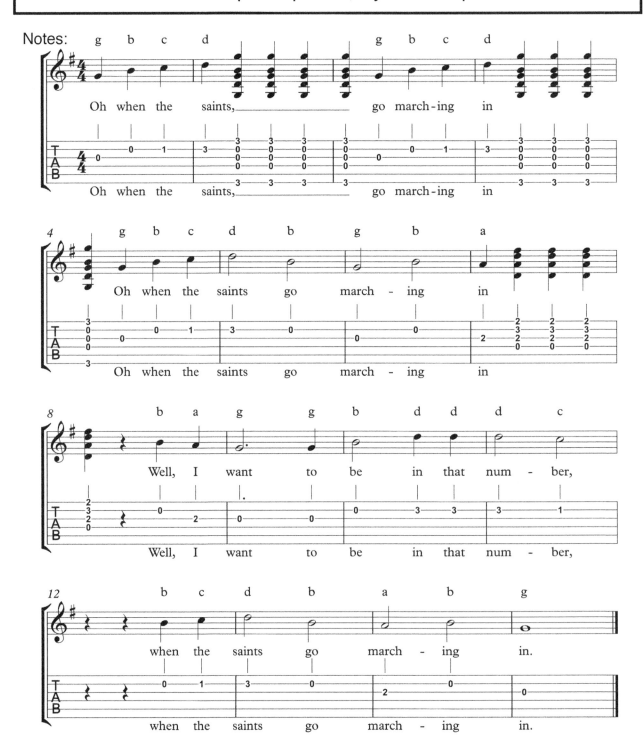

Lesson 31
Major Chords: Open Position

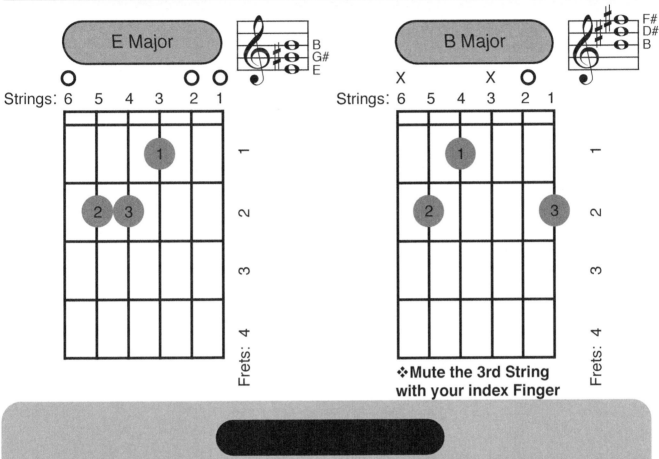

E Major

Strings: 6 5 4 3 2 1

Frets: 4

B Major

Strings: 6 5 4 3 2 1

Frets: 4

❖ **Mute the 3rd String with your index Finger**

Chord: (No Chord)	E	E	A
I've got	peace like a	river. I've got	Peace like a
Strum: 1 2 3 4	1 2 3 4	1 2 3 4	1 2 3 4
Chord: E	E	E	B
river. I've got	peace like a	river in my	soul.
Strum: 1 2 3 4	1 2 3 4	1 2 3 4	1 2 3 4
Chord: B	E	E	A
I've got	Peace like a	river. I've got	peace like a
Strum: 1 2 3 4	1 2 3 4	1 2 3 4	1 2 3 4
Chord: E	E	B	E
river. I've got	peace like a	river in my	soul.
Strum: 1 2 3 4	1 2 3 4	1 2 3 4	1 2 3 4

Lesson 32: The Melody for *Peace Like a River*

Here is another melody, in this case for *Peace Like a River*. This melody utilizes open strings to help facilitate ease of playing. **Have Fun!**

Peace Like a River

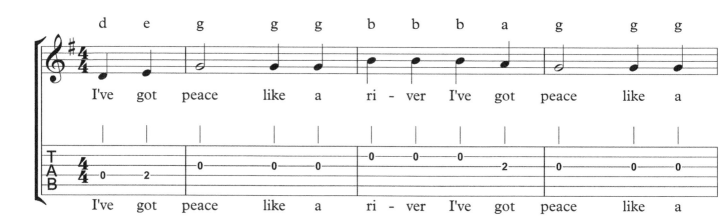

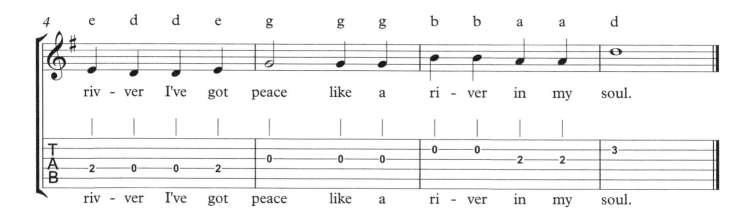

Try saying the note names as you play. Also, try playing without looking at your hands

Lesson 33
Let's Look Back:

D, G, & A Chords

+ Play though *When the Saints Go Marching In* using the D, G, & A major chords, instead of the C, F, and G major chords.

+ Go back to Lesson 21: *When the Saints Go Marching In*

+ When you see a C, play a D instead.

+ When you see a C7, play a D instead.

+ When you see a G, play an A instead.

+ When you see an F, play a G instead.

+ At first, try this very slowly.

C, F, & G Chords

+ *Play Amazing Grace* using the C, F, and G major chords, instead of D, G, and A major chords.

+ Go back to Lesson 18: *Amazing Grace*

+ When you see a D, play a C instead.

+ When you see a G, play an F instead.

+ When you see an A, play G instead.

+ At first, try this very slowly. Then, gradually increase the speed.

Major Chords

+ Find other songs that use these Major Chords.

+ Try playing through the songs in this section using different strumming patterns. For example, try these:

+ Down Up Down Up

+ Down Down Up Down

Have Fun!

Moving Forward

On the Following Pages:

Ⓡ Stands for Root

③ Stands for 3rd

⑤ Stands for 5th

O Means let the string vibrate

X Means mute the string with a Left-Hand Finger.

Before Moving Forward: Make sure that you are comfortable with the material you have learned so far. If not take a few days to review the material before moving to the next section of the book and videos.

Lesson 34
What We Have Learned So Far

- Open-Position Major Chords: A, B, C, D, E, F, G

- *Amazing Grace*

- *When the Saints Go Marching In*

- *Peace Like a River*

- The Structure of Major Chords

- The Structure of Minor Chords

- Basic Beats, Rhythms, and Strumming Patterns

Check Out These Artists Who Use Major Chords

- U2: *Where the Streets Have No Name*

- Bob Dylan: *Tangled Up in Blue*

- Bruno Mars: *Grenade*

- Lady Gaga: *Edge of Glory*

- The Cure: *Just Like Heaven*

Lesson 35: Overview
Major & Minor Chords

Intervals

+ Chords are formed by playing several different notes on the guitar at the same time.

+ The distances between these notes are called "intervals".

+ The most basic interval (or distance between notes) is called a "second".

+ There are 2 types of second intervals: minor and major.

+ On the guitar, the easiest way to understand these intervals is to look at the fretboard.

+ If you put one finger on the 1st fret and another on the 2nd fret, that is the distance of a minor second. If you put one finger on the 1st fret and another on the 3rd fret, that is the distance of a major second.

Major & Minor Chords

+ All Major & Minor Chords contain 3 notes: the Root, the 3rd, and the 5th.

+ In Major Chords the distance between the Root and the 3rd is made up of 2 Major 2nds.

+ In Minor Chords the distance between the Root and the 3rd is made up of 1 Major 2nd and 1 Minor 2nd.

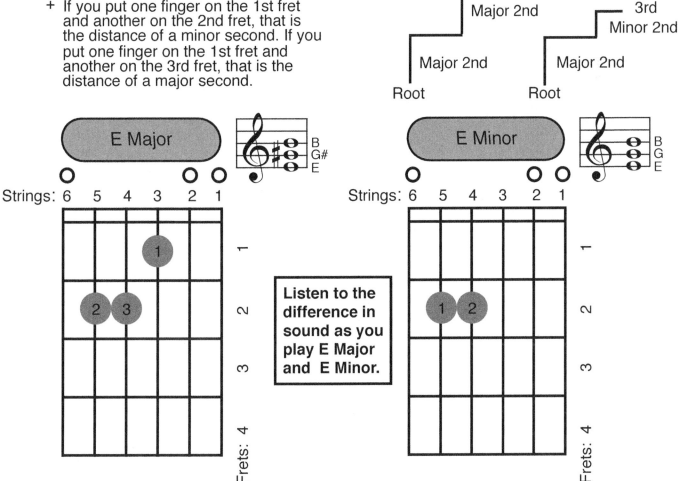

Listen to the difference in sound as you play E Major and E Minor.

Lesson 36
Minor Chords: Open Position

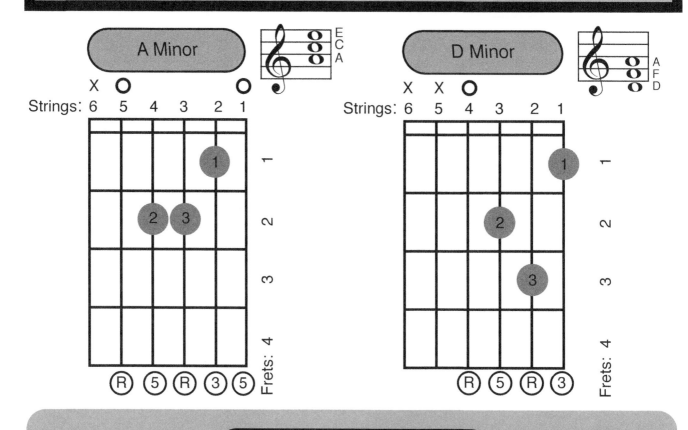

A Minor

E
C
A

Strings: 6 5 4 3 2 1
X O O

Frets: 4

R 5 R 3 5

D Minor

A
F
D

Strings: 6 5 4 3 2 1
X X O

Frets: 4

R 5 R 3

Chord:	**Am**	**C**	**D**	**F**
	There is a	house in	New Or-	leans they
Strum:	1 2 3	1 2 3	1 2 3	1 2 3

Chord:	**Am**	**C**	**E**	**E**
	call the	ris- ing	sun.	It's
Strum:	1 2 3	1 2 3	1 2 3	1 2 3

Chord:	**Am**	**C**	**D**	**F**
	been the	ruin of	many poor	souls and
Strum:	1 2 3	1 2 3	1 2 3	1 2 3

Chord:	**Am**	**E**	**Am**	**Am**
	Lord, I	know I'm	one.	
Strum:	1 2 3	1 2 3	1 2 3	1 2 3

Lesson 37: The Melody for
House of the Rising Sun

In this lesson, we are going to look at the melody for *House of the Rising Sun.* The melody, in this version, sits on the middle and lower strings. There are also a number of notes on the open strings of the guitar.

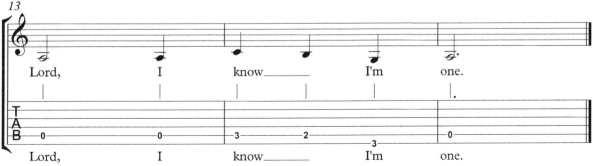

Lesson 38: Alternate Picking

Alternate picking is a technique where the guitarist "alternates" between playing notes with downstrokes and upstrokes of the pick. This allows for much more efficient picking than just moving the pick in one direction, for example, only picking down or only picking up. (For more information on alternate picking and other guitar techniques, you might want to check out *Guitar Scales Handbook*).

Here are two alternate-picking exercises (in tablature / TAB format) to improve your right-hand picking technique. Repeat each exercise at a comfortable tempo for between 1 and 2 minutes. If your hands start to feel tired, just shake them out and take a break for a while.

⊓ : This symbol stands for a downstroke.

V : This symbol stands for an upstroke.

```
    ⊓   V   ⊓   V   ⊓   V   ⊓   V
——— 0 — 1 — 0 — 1 — 0 — 1 — 0 — 1 ——— High-E String (1st String)
————————————————————————————————————— B String (2nd String)
————————————————————————————————————— G String (3rd String)
————————————————————————————————————— D String (4th String)
————————————————————————————————————— A String (5th String)
————————————————————————————————————— Low-E String (6th String)

    ⊓   V   ⊓   V   ⊓   V   ⊓   V
——— 1 — 2 — 1 — 2 — 1 — 2 — 1 — 2 ——— High-E String (1st String)
————————————————————————————————————— B String (2nd String)
————————————————————————————————————— G String (3rd String)
————————————————————————————————————— D String (4th String)
————————————————————————————————————— A String (5th String)
————————————————————————————————————— Low-E String (6th String)
```

Lesson 39
Minor Chords: Open Position

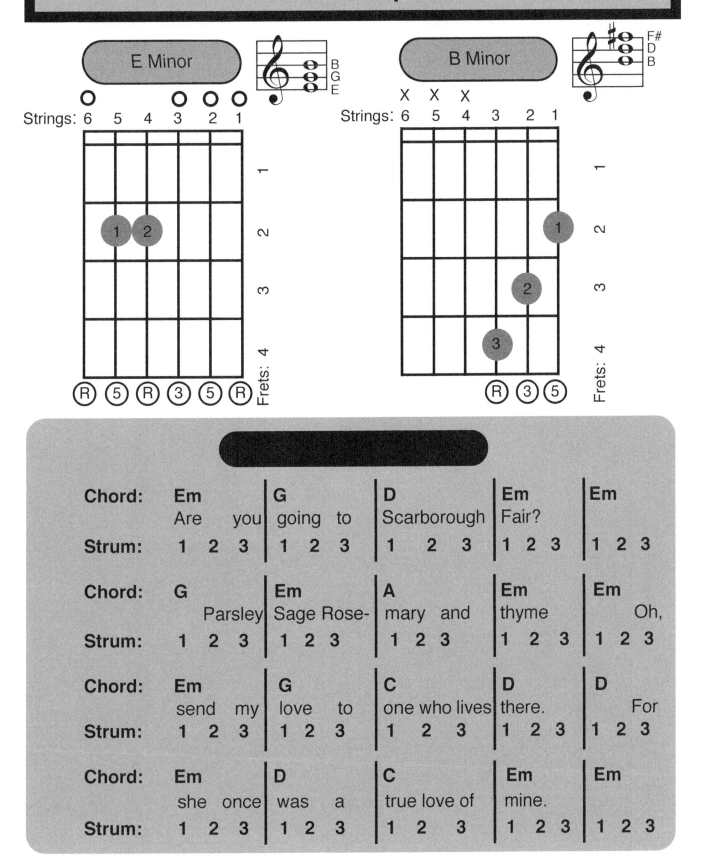

Chord:	Em	G	D	Em	Em
	Are you	going to	Scarborough	Fair?	
Strum:	1 2 3	1 2 3	1 2 3	1 2 3	1 2 3
Chord:	G	Em	A	Em	Em
	Parsley	Sage Rose-	mary and	thyme	Oh,
Strum:	1 2 3	1 2 3	1 2 3	1 2 3	1 2 3
Chord:	Em	G	C	D	D
	send my	love to	one who lives	there.	For
Strum:	1 2 3	1 2 3	1 2 3	1 2 3	1 2 3
Chord:	Em	D	C	Em	Em
	she once	was a	true love of	mine.	
Strum:	1 2 3	1 2 3	1 2 3	1 2 3	1 2 3

Lesson 40: The Melody for Scarborough Fair

Here is the melody for *Scarborough Fair*. It utilizes open strings and spans the middle to the upper strings of the guitar. Take your time to practice each line of music (called a "system"), before putting it all together.

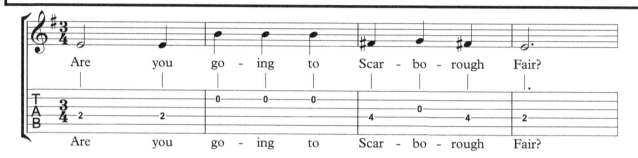

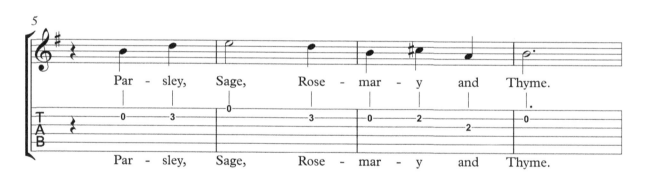

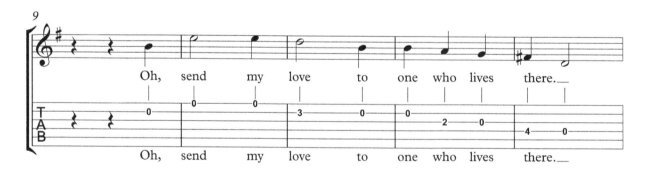

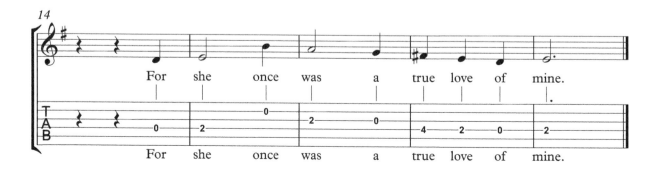

Lesson 41: Changing the Guitar Strings

Here is a nine-step method for changing your guitar strings:

Before starting, it's best to have a set of pliers and a string winder.

Step 1: Separate your strings and put them in order. You will be changing them one at a time.

Step 2: Loosen <u>one</u> string and snip it with your pliers. Do <u>not</u> cut all of your strings at once.

Step 3: Depending on your guitar model, feed the new string through the bridge from the back or side.

Step 4: Measure out a finger length of slack for the guitar string.

Step 5: Gently feed the string through the hole in the tuning peg.

Step 6: Make a downward-pointing fold in the string.

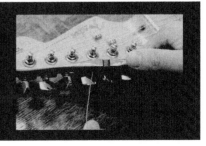

Step 7: Using the string winder, turn the tuning peg clockwise. This will tighten the string.

Step 8: Check to make sure that the string is wound upon itself. This will improve the tuning.

Step 9: Once the string is at the correct pitch, snip the excess wire with your pliers.

Lesson 42
Minor Chords: Open Position

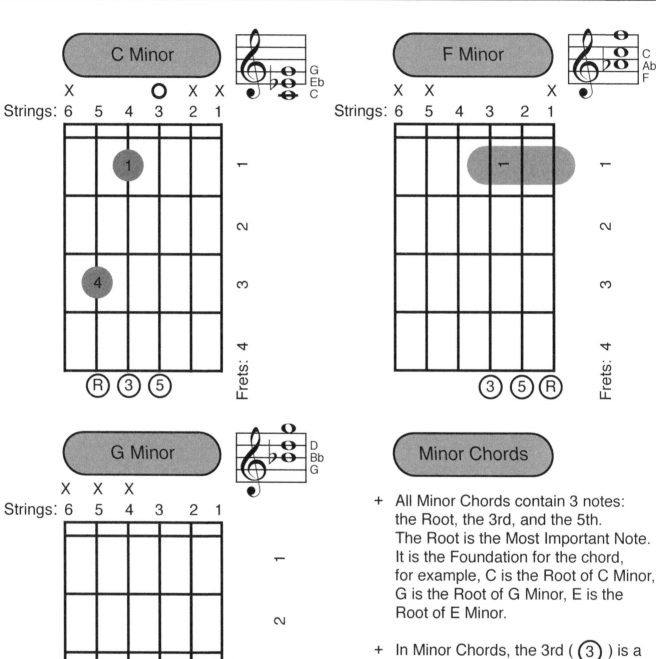

C Minor

X   O   X   X
Strings: 6   5   4   3   2   1

1

4

Ⓡ ③ ⑤

Frets: 4

G
Eb
C

F Minor

X   X   X
Strings: 6   5   4   3   2   1

1

③ ⑤ Ⓡ

Frets: 4

C
Ab
F

G Minor

X   X   X
Strings: 6   5   4   3   2   1

1

③ ⑤ Ⓡ

Frets: 4

D
Bb
G

Minor Chords

+ All Minor Chords contain 3 notes:
the Root, the 3rd, and the 5th.
The Root is the Most Important Note.
It is the Foundation for the chord,
for example, C is the Root of C Minor,
G is the Root of G Minor, E is the
Root of E Minor.

+ In Minor Chords, the 3rd (③) is a
1/2 step (1 Fret) lower than a Major
Chord. This lower 3rd in a Minor
Chord gives it the "Minor" sound
quality.

+ In general, Minor Chords have a
bittersweet or more somber character
than Major Chords (which tend to
sound brighter).

Lesson 43
Let's Look Back, Minor Chords:

E Minor

+ Play though *House of the Rising Sun* using the E Minor, A Minor, B, C, and G Major Chords.

+ Go back to Lesson 36: *House of the Rising Sun*

+ When you see Am, play a Em instead.

+ When you see a C, play an G instead.

+ When you see an F, play a C instead.

+ When you see an E, play a B instead.

+ At first, try this very slowly.

Strumming

+ As you Play through *House of the Rising Sun* using these different chords, try gently strumming the chords with the nails of your right-hand fingers.

+ Listen to the difference in sound between the fingernails and the pick.

+ Keep a loose wrist while strumming. This will give your chords a better sound and improve your rhythm.

+ If you have trouble making a transition to certain chords, isolate the 2 tricky chords. Then, alternate playing them very slowly.

Minor Chords

+ Find other songs that use these Minor Chords.

+ Try playing through *House of the Rising Sun* using different strumming patterns. For example, try these:

+ Down Up Down

+ Down Down Up

Have Fun!

Greensleeves

+ On the Following Page:

+ Greensleeves:

+ There are 3 strums (or beats) in each measure of Greensleeves.

+ The first beat of each measure is called the "downbeat".

+ Try to give more emphasis to the first strum ("downbeat") in each measure.

+ By slightly accenting the downbeat of each measure, you will provide a stronger rhythm to the song.

Lesson 44
Greensleeves

Verse Section

Chord:	Am	Am	G	G	Am
	A-las my	love, you	do me	wrong to	cast me
Strum:	1 2 3	1 2 3	1 2 3	1 2 3	1 2 3

Chord:	Am	E	E	Am	Am
	off dis-	courteous-	ly when	I have	loved
Strum:	1 2 3	1 2 3	1 2 3	1 2 3	1 2 3

Chord:	G	G	Am	E	Am
	you so	long, de-	light- ing	in your	com-pan-
Strum:	1 2 3	1 2 3	1 2 3	1 2 3	1 2 3

Chord:	Am	
	y	**Chorus Section (Go to the Next Line)**
Strum:	1 2 3	

Chord:	C	C	G	G
	Green	Sleeves was	all my	joy and
Strum:	1 2 3	1 2 3	1 2 3	1 2 3

Chord:	Am	Am	E	E
	Green	Sleeves was	my de-	light.
Strum:	1 2 3	1 2 3	1 2 3	1 2 3

Chord:	C	C	G	G
	Green	Sleeves was	heart of	gold and
Strum:	1 2 3	1 2 3	1 2 3	1 2 3

Chord:	Am	E	Am	Am
	who but my	lady	Green	Sleeves.
Strum:	1 2 3	1 2 3	1 2 3	1 2 3

Lesson 45: The Melody for Greensleeves (Chorus Section)

This is the melody for the chorus section of *Greensleeves.* Most of the notes sit on the top three strings of the guitar: High-E, B, and G.

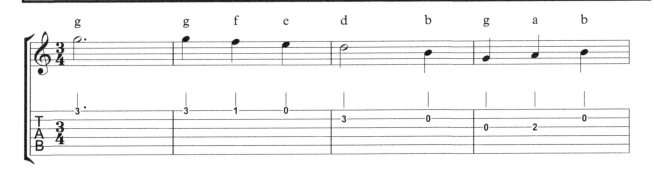

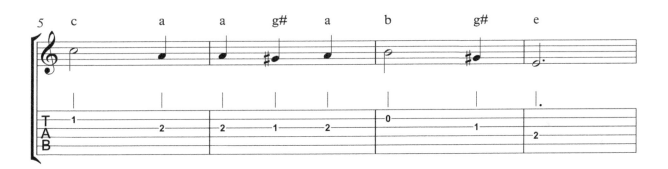

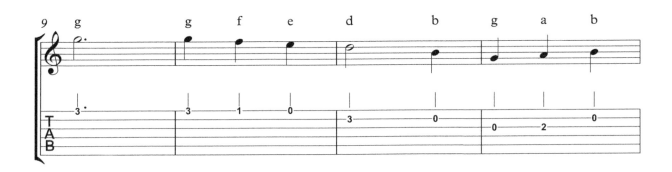

Lesson 46
What We Have Learned So Far

- Open-Position Minor Chords: A, B, C, D, E, F, G

- *House of the Rising Sun*

- *Scarborough Fair*

- *Greensleeves*

- The Structure of Minor Chords, continued

- Combining Major and Minor Chords in the Same Song

Check Out These Artists Who Use Minor Chords

- The Beatles: *Eleanor Rigby*

- Bruce Springsteen: *The River*

- Foo Fighters: *Walk*

- Aerosmith: *Dream On*

Lesson 47:
Blues Guitar Basics

From Eric Clapton to Greg Allman to Jimi Hendrix to Stevie Ray Vaughan to Bonnie Raitt, so many great guitarists have been inspired by the Blues.

In these next few lessons, we are going to look at Blues techniques, licks, chords, and progressions that will add some style and spice to your playing. These techniques and ideas are the starting points for a course of nearly endless musical discovery. So, take your time with this material and have fun enjoying the process!

Part of becoming a good guitarist is discovering your own musical voice. One way to grow this way, as a musician, is to look for different ways to play the materials presented in this book. Try changing the angle of your guitar pick or pluck the notes in different sections of the string. You will hear how these little variations create a considerably different sound on your instrument.

On the next page, we are going to look at our first Dominant 7th chords. These are chords that are frequently used in Rock, Blues, Jazz, Country and many other styles of music. They are similar to major chords, but have one extra note, which is called a "seventh". In technical terms, the seventh of a Dominant 7th chord is a Minor 7th interval above the Root note of the chord. (If you don't remember what an interval is, check out the lesson on intervals from earlier in the book.)

For an A Dominant Seventh chord, the note "A" is the Root and the note "G" is the 7th of the chord (the note that is a Minor 7th interval above the Root note "A"). For a D Dominant Seventh chord, the note "D" is the Root and the note "C" is the 7th of the chord (the note that is a Minor 7th interval above the Root note "D"). Finally, for an E Dominant Seventh chord, the note "E" is the Root and the note "D" is the 7th of the chord (the note that is a Minor 7th interval above the Root note "E").

Dominant Seventh chords are abbreviated by using the letter name of the chord and the number seven. For example an A Dominant Seventh chord would be abbreviated this way: A7. An E Dominant Seventh chord would be abbreviated this way: E7.

In the chart below, you will find depictions of the A7, D7, and E7 chords. The letter names of the notes of the chords and their interval positioning are included in the diagram.

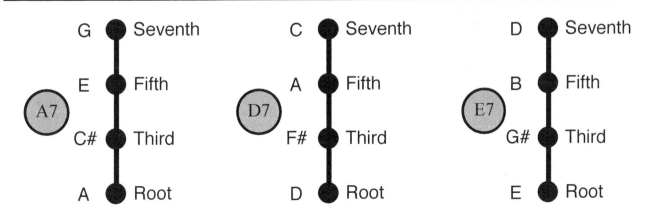

Lesson 48: Dominant 7th Chords Open Position

❖Check Out Video Lesson 5

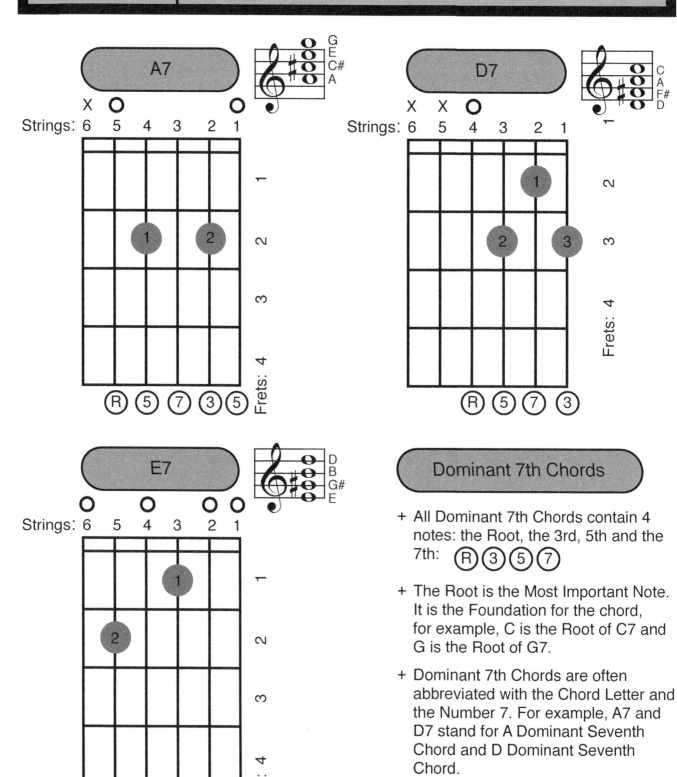

Dominant 7th Chords

+ All Dominant 7th Chords contain 4 notes: the Root, the 3rd, 5th and the 7th: Ⓡ③⑤⑦

+ The Root is the Most Important Note. It is the Foundation for the chord, for example, C is the Root of C7 and G is the Root of G7.

+ Dominant 7th Chords are often abbreviated with the Chord Letter and the Number 7. For example, A7 and D7 stand for A Dominant Seventh Chord and D Dominant Seventh Chord.

+ Dominant 7th Chords have a "bluesy" quality and can "spice" up Major Chords.

Lesson 49: Music Theory
What are Chord Progressions?

In all major and minor scales, we give the notes numbers based on their position. These numbers go from one to seven. In music, we call these numbers "scale degrees". The numbers are often written as Roman Numerals (see chart below).

The root (the main note of the scale) is always number (or degree) one. In the key of C, which is the white keys of the piano, the notes are C, D, E, F, G, A, and B. Each one of these notes is given a number from 1 to 7. Basically, the numbers just start from the root note, which is number one, and go up in order to seven. So, it's pretty simple and doesn't require any advanced math skills.

Here are the Notes and Corresponding Numbers for the Scale Degrees in the Key of C Major. The Roman Numerals for Each Scale Degree are written on the Right.

C = 1 = I
D = 2 = II
E = 3 = III
F = 4 = IV
G = 5 = V
A = 6 = VI
B = 7 = VII

A chord progression is just a fancy term that means a group of chords that follows a particular pattern. These patterns often repeat several times during a song. In Rock, Blues, Country, Metal, Folk, and Pop there are several chord progressions that are very common. You have probably heard these progressions hundreds of times.

Chord progressions are given names based on the scale degree numbers of the root notes of the chords. For instance, a chord progression in C Major that features only the chords C, F, and G is called a I, IV, V progression--pronounced like this: a one, four, five progression. Refer to the chart above and on the right for the scale degrees.

Below is a graphic representation of the scale degrees in C Major. The scale degrees are written as Roman Numerals at the bottom of the diagram.

Letter Names:	C	D	E	F	G	A	B	C
Scale Degrees:	I	II	III	IV	V	VI	VII	I

Lesson 50: Twelve-Bar Blues In the Key of A

In A

Chord: A7	A7	A7	A7
Strum: 1 2 3 4	1 2 3 4	1 2 3 4	1 2 3 4

Chord: D7	D7	A7	A7
Strum: 1 2 3 4	1 2 3 4	1 2 3 4	1 2 3 4

Chord: E7	D7	A7	A7
Strum: 1 2 3 4	1 2 3 4	1 2 3 4	1 2 3 4

Twelve-Bar Blues

In music the word "bar" means "measure". Many Blues, Rock, and Jazz songs use a twelve-measure (or "12-Bar") format. For this format, you play the 12 measures and then return to the beginning and repeat them again. So, as you play music with family and friends, you might hear some of them use the expression "Twelve-Bar Blues" and you will know what they mean. Some famous examples of Twelve-Bar Blues are *Crossroads* by Eric Clapton and *Pride and Joy* by Stevie Ray Vaughan.

Most Twelve-Bar Blues follow a I, IV, V progression (that is, a "one, four, five progression"). The Twelve-Bar Blues song in this lesson is in the key of A. So, the A7 chord is the I chord ("the one chord"). The D7 chord is the IV chord ("the four chord"). The E7 chord is the V chord ("the five chord"). Once you learn this song, try it out with the Play-Along Video.

After you have played through the "12-Bar Blues" a few times with 4 strums per measure, try experimenting with different strumming patterns and rhythms. ***Have Fun!***

Lesson 51: Rockabilly Groove, Overview

Rockabilly is a mix of Blues, Rock, Jazz and Country. It was popularized in the 1950s by artists like Elvis and Chuck Berry. Two good examples of the style are *Hound Dog* by Elvis and *Johnny Be Good* by Chuck Berry. Take a few minutes today and check out recordings of these songs on Youtube. You might also like to hear *Rock This Town* by the Stray Cats.

❖**Check Out Video 6**

Our Rockabilly Lessons (on the next few pages) involve chord patterns played on only 2 adjacent strings. When playing these lessons, try to isolate each 2-string chord and make short strums with your Right Hand. Check out the video lesson to see and hear how this technique works.

The example below shows the basic pattern. For this example, only play the 5th and 4th strings (the A & D strings). Use your index finger (1st finger) for the notes on the second fret. For notes on the fourth fret, try to use your ring finger (3rd finger). If this is too much of a stretch, try using your pinky (4th finger) to play the notes on the fourth fret.

For the Rockabilly material on the next few pages, take your time and master each two-string pattern. Then, slowly try linking them together. First try linking the A Riff and the D Riff.

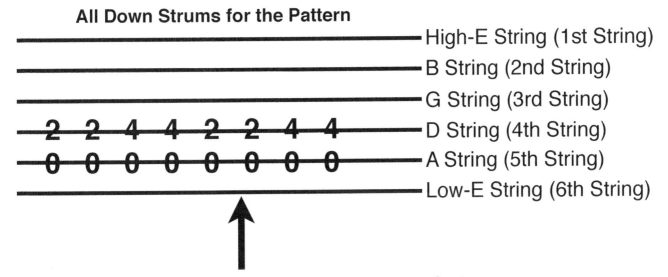

All Down Strums for the Pattern

High-E String (1st String)
B String (2nd String)
G String (3rd String)
D String (4th String)
A String (5th String)
Low-E String (6th String)

Play all of these notes on the 4th & 5th Strings.

Lesson 52:
Rockabilly Progression, Part 1

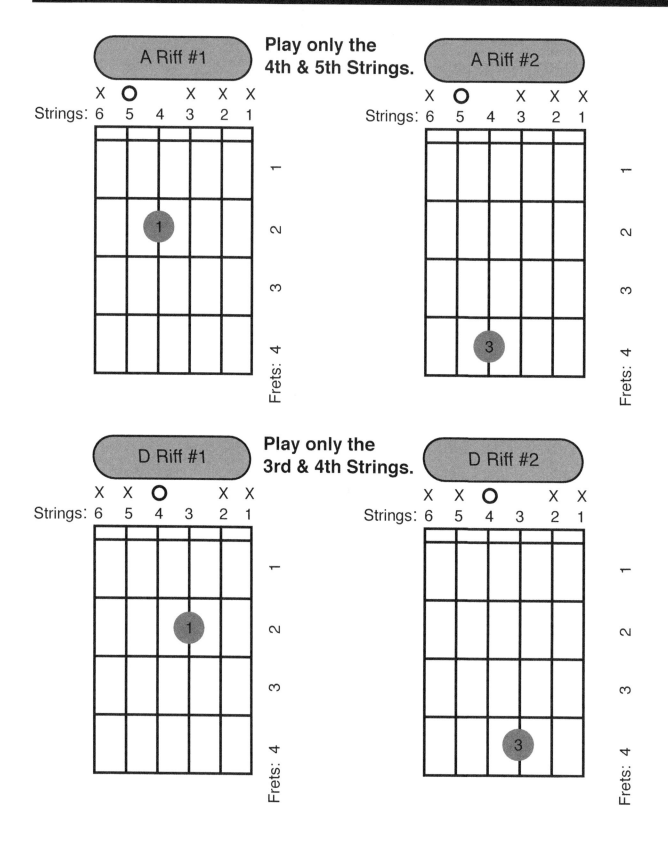

Play only the 4th & 5th Strings.

A Riff #1

A Riff #2

Play only the 3rd & 4th Strings.

D Riff #1

D Riff #2

Lesson 53:
Rockabilly Progression, Part 2

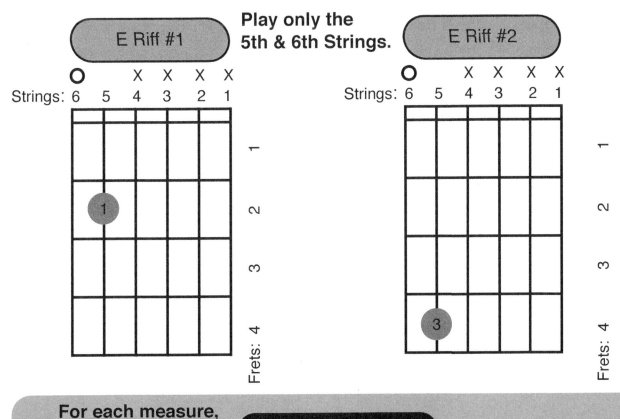

E Riff #1

Play only the 5th & 6th Strings.

E Riff #2

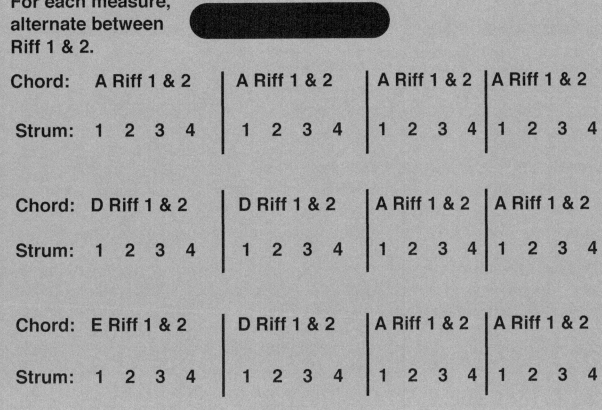

For each measure, alternate between Riff 1 & 2.

Chord:	A Riff 1 & 2	A Riff 1 & 2	A Riff 1 & 2	A Riff 1 & 2
Strum:	1 2 3 4	1 2 3 4	1 2 3 4	1 2 3 4
Chord:	D Riff 1 & 2	D Riff 1 & 2	A Riff 1 & 2	A Riff 1 & 2
Strum:	1 2 3 4	1 2 3 4	1 2 3 4	1 2 3 4
Chord:	E Riff 1 & 2	D Riff 1 & 2	A Riff 1 & 2	A Riff 1 & 2
Strum:	1 2 3 4	1 2 3 4	1 2 3 4	1 2 3 4

Lesson 54: Secret to Guitar Success #4: Listen to Music Outside Your Comfort Zone

This week, as you work on improving your guitar playing and musicianship, have a little fun by listening to some genres and styles of music outside of your regular listening comfort zone. The best musicians often have a broad knowledge of music and can draw inspiration from many styles.

By exposing yourself to new artists and genres you will grow in new and unexpected ways as a guitarist. For instance, if you are a Blues fan and try listening to a few Classical recordings, you might get some new ideas for sound colors and textures on the electric guitar. If you are a Metal player and listen to some Jazz recordings, you might get some new ideas for riffs and rhythms.

Online there are a number of streaming music services that offer a free version. Spotify and Pandora are the most popular at the moment. You might also do some genre searches on Youtube. *Have Fun!*

Lesson 55: Secret to Guitar Success #5: Listen to Yourself

Every few days or once a week, record yourself playing some of your favorite songs or licks. You don't need to have an expensive recording device. If you have a microphone and some dictation or recording software on your phone, tablet or computer, those will work as well.

These recordings do not need to be high fidelity. The purpose of recording yourself is to listen to your playing from an "outside" perspective. When you press the playback, pay attention to your rhythm, the evenness of your tone and playing, and your expression. Every week, try to make slight improvements in these areas.

Have a positive and constructive attitude when you are listening to these recordings. Try not to get hung up on small details or little mistakes. Instead, listen to any awkward patterns or habits in your playing and work on improving in those areas.

As a side benefit, this practice will also get you used to the process of recording. So, if you are ever in a recording studio or at a friend's house making a recording, the process will not feel that unusual to you. You will be right at home.

Lesson 56: A Word about Scales & the Blues Scale

- Scales are groups of notes arranged in stepwise patterns, either going up or down. The combination of these steps (also called "intervals") gives each type of scale its unique sound and character.
- On this page, we are going to start learning about the Blues Scale: one of the most popular scales that is used in Rock, Pop, Country, and Folk.

- The Blues Scale (also called "Pentatonic Minor") is a 5-Note Scale that is used in Rock, Jazz, Pop, Country, and Blues songs.
- Take a look at the chart below. It displays the 5 notes of the Blues Scale in the key of A. In the key of A, the notes are A, C, D, E, and G.
- On your guitar, locate the 5th String (the second thickest string). Play the notes of the scale pattern from the chart below and listen to the character of the sound.
- Also, try to make little melodies ("licks") with the Blues scale notes.

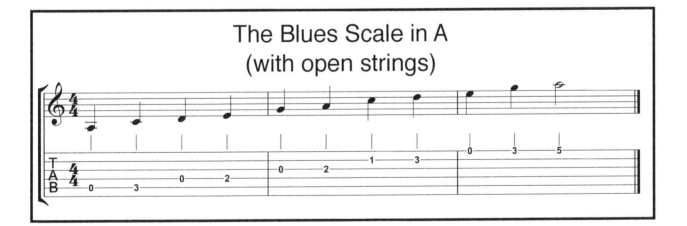

The Blues Scale in A
(with open strings)

- Take some time this week to listen to Blues Music.
- What are some of the musical characteristics of the style?
- What combinations of instruments are used in the songs?
- What techniques do the singers use to give a little musical "spice" to the vocal lines? Can these ideas be transferred to guitar playing?

Lesson 57: The Blues Licks in A: Using Open Strings

Here are four guitar licks that use open strings in the A Blues Scale. Try them one at a time using fingers number one and two of your left hand.

You can use these Blues licks (and variations on them) to make guitar solos and improvisations over the Rockabilly play-along video.

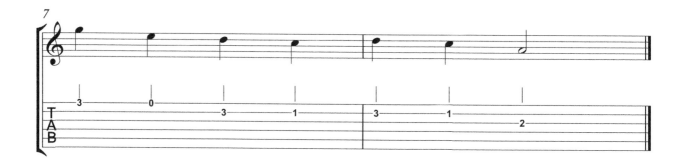

Lesson 58: Dominant 7th Chords
Open Position

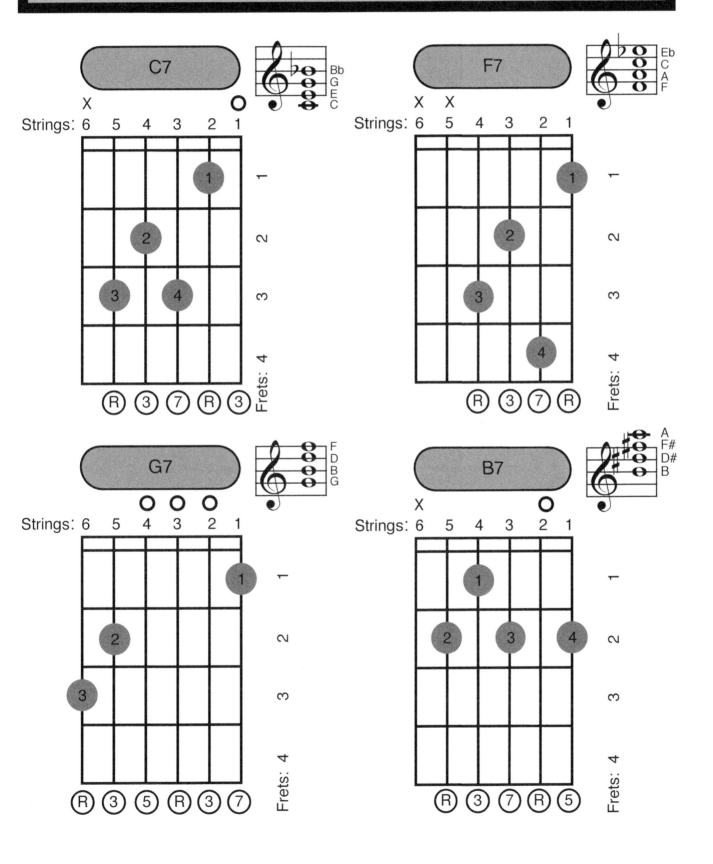

Lesson 59
12-Bar Blues Progression

In C

Chord:	C7	C7	C7	C7
Strum: (Beat)	1 2 3 4	1 2 3 4	1 2 3 4	1 2 3 4

Chord:	F7	F7	C7	C7
Strum: (Beat)	1 2 3 4	1 2 3 4	1 2 3 4	1 2 3 4

Chord:	G7	F7	C7	C7
Strum: (Beat)	1 2 3 4	1 2 3 4	1 2 3 4	1 2 3 4

Blues in C

+ Here is a 12-Bar Blues in the key of C.

+ First, try strumming for all 4 beats in each measure.

+ Next, try strumming only the 1st beat of each measure, while counting the beats aloud or in your head. For example, count "1, 2, 3, 4, 1, 2, 3, 4, 1, 2, 3, 4..." until you get to the end of the song.

+ Finally, try the exercise mentioned above, but strum on the 1st and 3rd beats, while counting aloud or in your head.

Dominant 7ths

+ Find other songs that use these Dominant 7th Chords.

+ Try playing through the songs in this section using different strumming patterns. For example, try these:

+ Down Up Down Up

Have Fun!

Lesson 60
What We Have Learned So Far

- Open-Position Dominant Seventh Chords:

  A, B, C, D, E, F, G

- *12-Bar Blues in A*

- *Rockabilly Progression*

- *12-Bar Blues in C*

- The Structure of Dominant Seventh Chords

- New Rhythms and Strumming Patterns

Check Out These Artists Who Use Dominant 7th Chords

- Stevie Ray Vaughn: *Texas Flood*

- Eric Clapton: *Crossroads*

- B.B. King: *The Thrill is Gone*

- Stray Cats: *Stray Cat Strut*

Lesson 61: Basic Guitar Strumming Patterns

Here are four examples of basic guitar strumming patterns. All of the examples are in 4/4 time; so, you should count "1 & 2 & 3 & 4 &" for each measure. The "&" (or "and") stands for the upbeat (the halfway point for each beat). The down arrows represent down strums and the up arrows represent up strums. Try strumming a C Major chord using these different patterns. Listen to the way each one sounds.

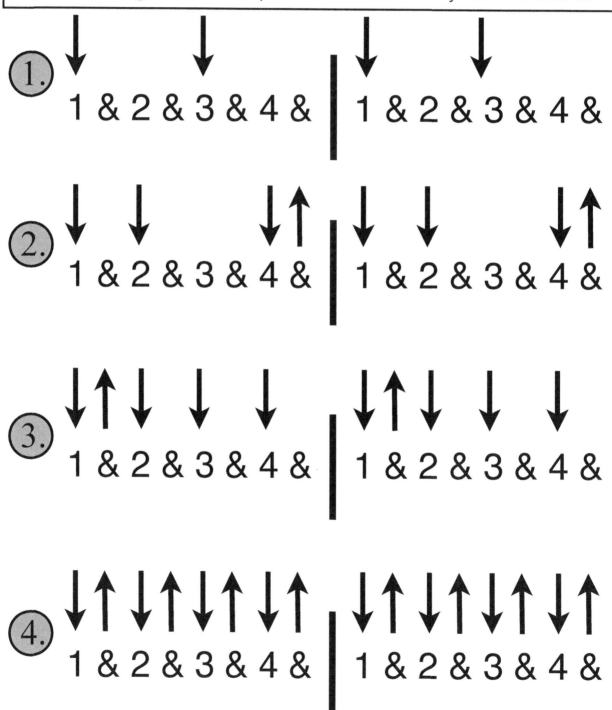

Lesson 62: Minor 7th Chords
Open Position

❖Check Out
Video Lesson 7

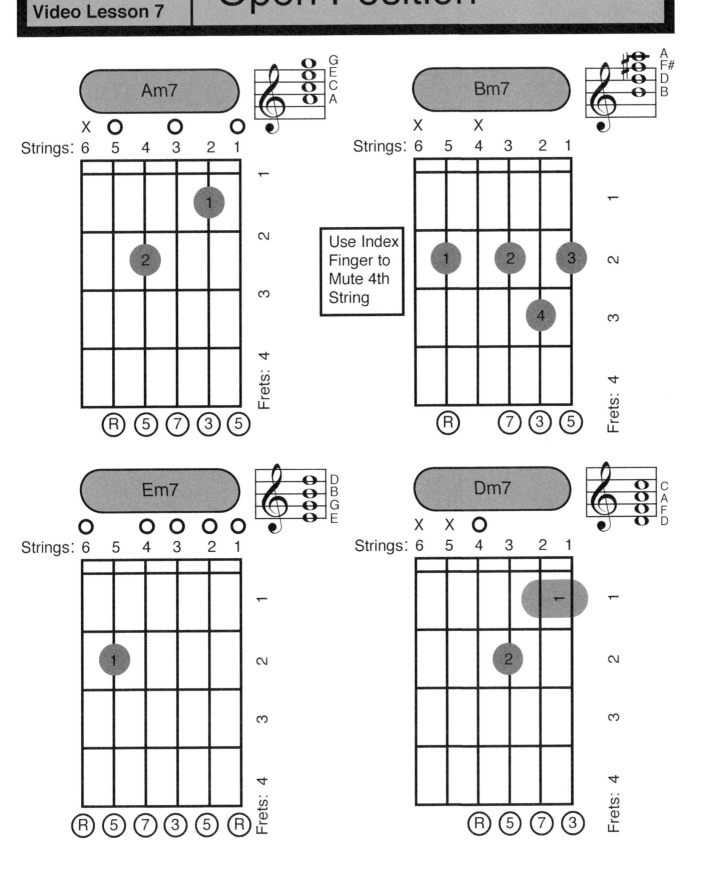

Lesson 63
Jazz / Pop Progression

Chord:	D	Bm7	Em7	A7
Beat:	1 2 3 4	1 2 3 4	1 2 3 4	1 2 3 4

Chord:	D	Bm7	Em7	A7
Beat:	1 2 3 4	1 2 3 4	1 2 3 4	1 2 3 4

Chord:	G7	F7	C7	C7
Beat:	1 2 3 4	1 2 3 4	1 2 3 4	1 2 3 4

Minor 7th Chords

+ All Minor 7th Chords contain 4 notes: the Root, the 3rd, 5th and the 7th:

Ⓡ ③ ⑤ ⑦

+ The Root is the Most Important Note. It is the Foundation for the chord, for example, C is the Root of Cm7 and G is the Root of Gm7.

+ Minor 7th Chords are often abbreviated with the Chord Letter and the Number 7. For example, Am7 and Dm7 stand for A Minor Seventh Chord and D Minor Seventh Chord.

Jazz Style

+ Minor 7th Chords are very common in Jazz.

+ For *Jazz in D*, try strumming each beat lightly with the pick.

+ For a different sound, try strumming with the side of your thumb.

+ To give a different sound color to the chords, try strumming along various locations of the neck, for example, near the bridge, over the pickups or sound hole, or near where the neck meets the body.

Lesson 64: Secret to Guitar Success #6: Keep an Open Mind

Each day, try to draw inspiration for your guitar playing from the world around you. It might be things as varied as the combinations of sounds from many simultaneous conversations that you hear at a cafeteria or the rhythmic, cloud-like motion of flock of birds. Metaphorically speaking, keep your eyes and ears open to the things happening around you. You never know what small thing might turn into a big inspiration.

Lesson 65: Secret to Guitar Success #7: From Time to Time, Try New Gear

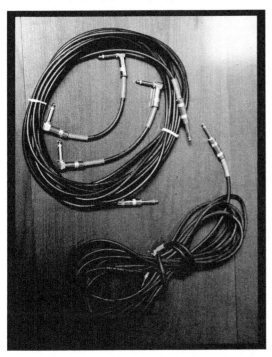

From time to time, you should try out new gear on your guitar. For the most part, this will entail changing things that are not expensive. For instance, you might try using a thinner or thicker guitar pick. Just by making this small modification to your playing, you will change the character of your sound. You might also try using a different brand or gauge ("thickness") of strings. Different brands of cables, if you are playing with an electric guitar and amplifier, will also affect the sound of your guitar in many substantial ways. You might also talk to friends and family members who play the guitar and ask them about what guitar picks, strings, and cables that they use on their instruments.

All of these above-mentioned examples are either free or inexpensive. So, before you decide that you need a new amp or guitar, try changing some of the elements listed above. You might be pleasantly surprised by the results.

Lesson 66: Minor 7th Chords Open Position

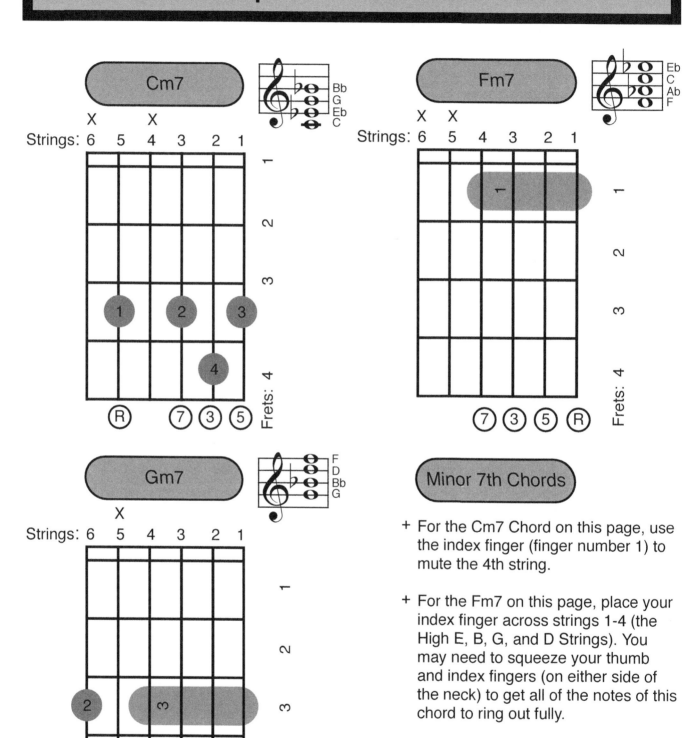

Cm7

Bb
G
Eb
C

X ⠀⠀⠀ X
Strings: 6 5 4 3 2 1

1 ⠀ 2 ⠀ 3

2 ⠀ 3

3

4 ⠀⠀ Frets: 4

Ⓡ ⠀ ⑦③⑤

Fm7

Eb
C
Ab
F

X ⠀ X
Strings: 6 5 4 3 2 1

1

1

2

3

Frets: 4

⑦③⑤Ⓡ

Gm7

F
D
Bb
G

X
Strings: 6 5 4 3 2 1

1

2

2 ⠀ 3 ⠀⠀ 3

Frets: 4

Ⓡ ⠀ ⑦③⑤Ⓡ

Use 1st Finger to Mute 5th String

Minor 7th Chords

+ For the Cm7 Chord on this page, use the index finger (finger number 1) to mute the 4th string.

+ For the Fm7 on this page, place your index finger across strings 1-4 (the High E, B, G, and D Strings). You may need to squeeze your thumb and index fingers (on either side of the neck) to get all of the notes of this chord to ring out fully.

+ For the Gm7 Chord on this page, use your middle finger (finger number 2) to mute the 5th string. Place your ring finger (finger number 3) across strings 1-4 (the High E, B, G, and D Strings).

Lesson 67: CM7 & FM7
Jazz / Pop Progression #2

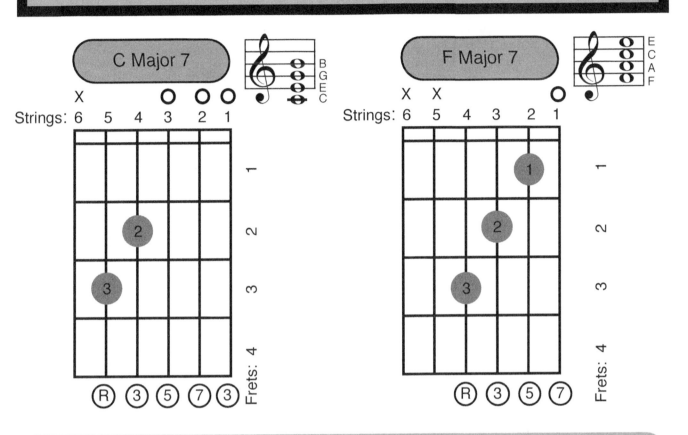

C Major 7

X   O   O   O
Strings: 6 5 4 3 2 1

Frets: 1 2 3 4

Ⓡ ③ ⑤ ⑦ ③

B
G
E
C

F Major 7

X   X   O
Strings: 6 5 4 3 2 1

Frets: 1 2 3 4

Ⓡ ③ ⑤ ⑦

E
C
A
F

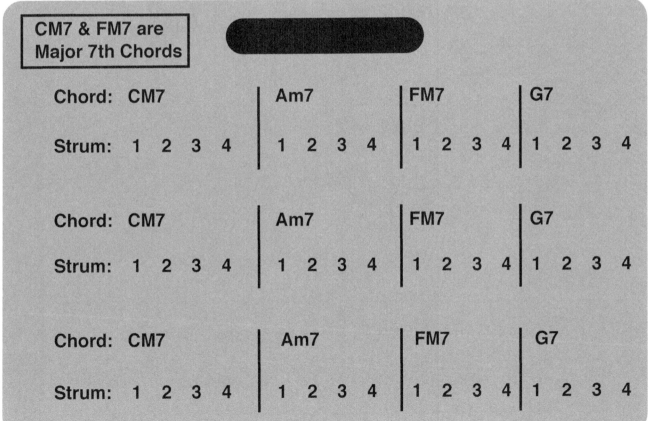

CM7 & FM7 are Major 7th Chords

Chord: CM7	Am7	FM7	G7
Strum: 1 2 3 4	1 2 3 4	1 2 3 4	1 2 3 4
Chord: CM7	Am7	FM7	G7
Strum: 1 2 3 4	1 2 3 4	1 2 3 4	1 2 3 4
Chord: CM7	Am7	FM7	G7
Strum: 1 2 3 4	1 2 3 4	1 2 3 4	1 2 3 4

Lesson 68
Jazz Minor Blues Progression

in A minor

Chord:	Am7				Am7				Dm7				Am7			
	Sometimes I				feel	like a			motherless				child.			
Strum:	1	2	3	4	1	2	3	4	1	2	3	4	1	2	3	4

Chord:	Dm7				Dm7				E7				Am7			
	Sometimes I				feel	like a			motherless				child.			
Strum:	1	2	3	4	1	2	3	4	1	2	3	4	1	2	3	4

Chord:	Am7				Am7				Dm7				Am7			
	Sometimes I				feel	like a			motherless				child.			A-
Strum:	1	2	3	4	1	2	3	4	1	2	3	4	1	2	3	4

Chord:	FM7				Am7				E7				Am7			
	long				way	from	home.									A-
Strum:	1	2	3	4	1	2	3	4	1	2	3	4	1	2	3	4

Chord:	FM7				Am7				E7				Am7			
	long				way	from	home.									
Strum:	1	2	3	4	1	2	3	4	1	2	3	4	1	2	3	4

1. Try strumming on all 4 beats of each measure.

2. Next, try strumming on only the first beat of each measure.

Lesson 69: The Melody for *Sometimes I Feel Like a Motherless Child*

In this lesson, we are going to play the melody for *Sometimes I Feel Like a Motherless Child.* Take your time to work out the rhythm for the song.

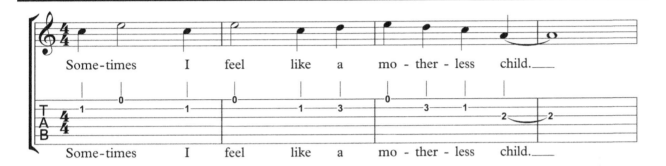

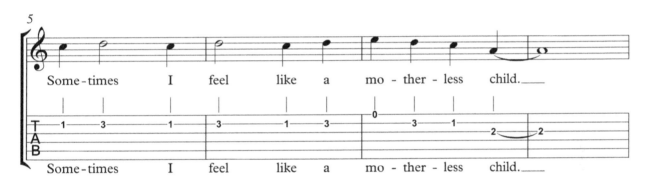

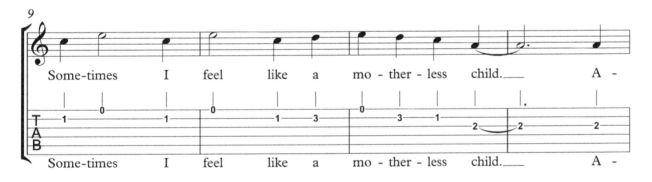

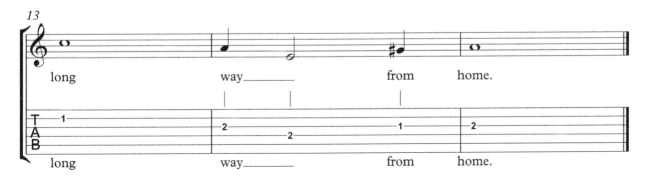

Lesson 70:
What We Have Learned So Far

- Open-Position Minor Seventh Chords:

  A, B, C, D, E, F, G

- *Jazz / Pop Progression*

- *Jazz in C*

- *Sometimes I Feel Like a Motherless Child*

- The Structure of Minor Seventh Chords

- New Strumming Patterns

Check Out These Artists Who Use Minor 7th Chords

- Jimi Hendrix: *Little Wing*

- Danny Gatton: *In My Room*

- Steely Dan: *Kid Charlemagne*

- Dave Matthews Band: *The Best of What's Around*

Lesson 71:
Notes on the 3rd String

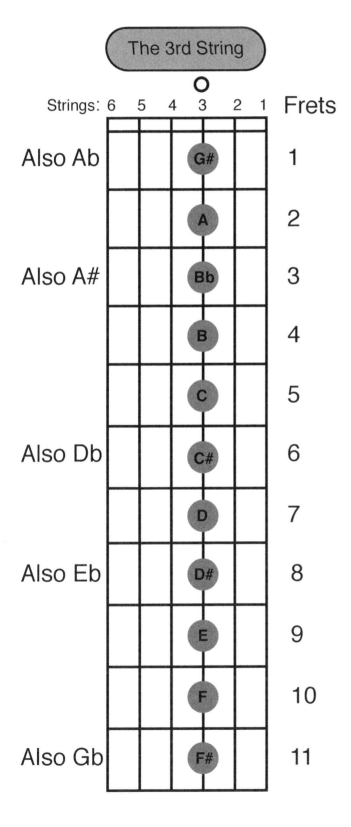

The 3rd String

Strings: 6 5 4 3 2 1   Frets

	Fret	
	G#	1
Also Ab		
	A	2
Also A#	Bb	3
	B	4
	C	5
Also Db	C#	6
	D	7
Also Eb	D#	8
	E	9
	F	10
Also Gb	F#	11

Notes on the 3rd String

+ It is good to think of the guitar neck as a series of horizontal and vertical lines.

+ In our book diagrams, the vertical lines are the strings. The horizontal lines are the frets.

+ If you play the 3rd String, (marked with a O in the 3rd-String Chart on the right of this page), the note "G" will sound.

+ If you put a finger on the 1st fret of the 3rd String, the note "G#" will sound.

+ The Sharps (#) and Flats (b) are notes that occur between the Natural notes: A,B,C,D,E,F & G.

+ The Sharps and Flats are the Black Keys on a Piano.

+ The Natural Notes are the White Keys on a Piano.

+ Each Sharp can also be called a Flat, for example "C#" is also "Db" and "F#" can be called "Gb".

+ In the same way, each Flat can also be called a Sharp, for example "Eb" can be called "D#" and "Ab" can be called "G#".

+ **Look at the chart on the right and try to find the notes on the 3rd string of your guitar neck.**

Lesson 72: 3-Note Moveable Major Chords from the 3rd String

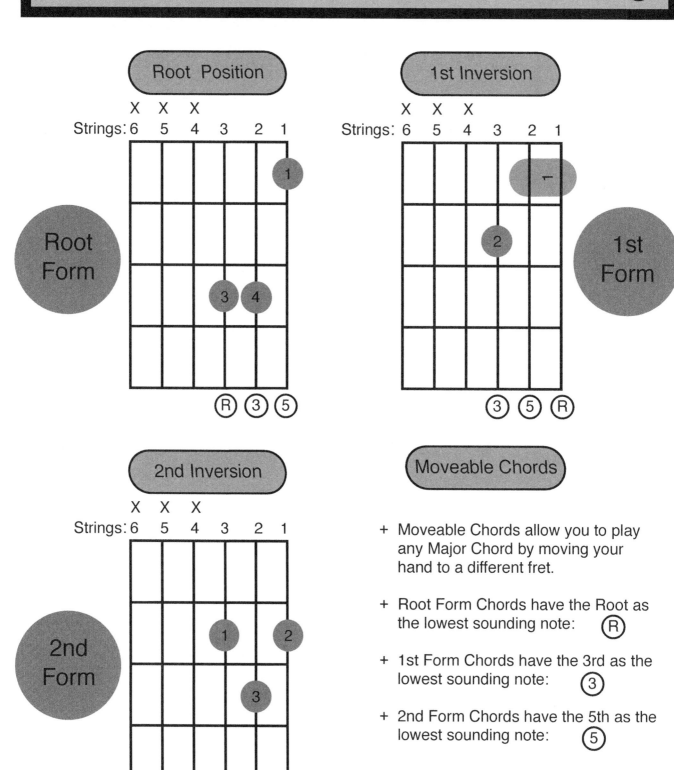

Root Position

Strings: 6 5 4 3 2 1

Root Form

1st Inversion

Strings: 6 5 4 3 2 1

1st Form

2nd Inversion

Strings: 6 5 4 3 2 1

2nd Form

Moveable Chords

+ Moveable Chords allow you to play any Major Chord by moving your hand to a different fret.

+ Root Form Chords have the Root as the lowest sounding note: Ⓡ

+ 1st Form Chords have the 3rd as the lowest sounding note: ③

+ 2nd Form Chords have the 5th as the lowest sounding note: ⑤

Lesson 73: *Amazing Grace*
Using only 2nd Form Chords

Fret:	2nd (with Index Finger)	2nd	7th	2nd
Chord:	D	D	G	D
	A-mazing	Grace how	sweet the	sound that
Strum:	1 2 3	1 2 3	1 2 3	1 2 3

Fret:	2nd	2nd	9th	9th
Chord:	D	D	A	A
	saved a	wretch like	me.	I
Strum:	1 2 3	1 2 3	1 2 3	1 2 3

Fret:	2nd	2nd	7th	2nd
Chord:	D	D	G	D
	once was	lost but	now am	found. Was
Strum:	1 2 3	1 2 3	1 2 3	1 2 3

Fret:	2nd	9th	2nd	2nd
Chord:	D	A	D	D
	blind but	now I	see.	
Strum:	1 2 3	1 2 3	1 2 3	1 2 3

Lesson 74: *Amazing Grace* Using All 3 Chord Forms

in D

(with Index Finger)

Fret:	5th	5th	7th	5th
Form:	Root	Root	2nd	Root
Chord:	D	D	G	D
	A-mazing	Grace how	sweet the	sound that
Strum:	1 2 3	1 2 3	1 2 3	1 2 3

Fret:	5th	5th	5th	5th
Form:	Root	Root	1st	1st
Chord:	D	D	A	A
	saved a	wretch like	me.	I
Strum:	1 2 3	1 2 3	1 2 3	1 2 3

Fret:	5th	5th	7th	5th
Form:	Root	Root	2nd	Root
Chord:	D	D	G	D
	once was	lost but	now am	found. Was
Strum:	1 2 3	1 2 3	1 2 3	1 2 3

Fret:	5th	5th	5th	5th
Form:	Root	1st	Root	Root
Chord:	D	A	D	D
	blind but	now I	see.	
Strum:	1 2 3	1 2 3	1 2 3	1 2 3

Lesson 75:
Notes on the 4th String

The 4th String

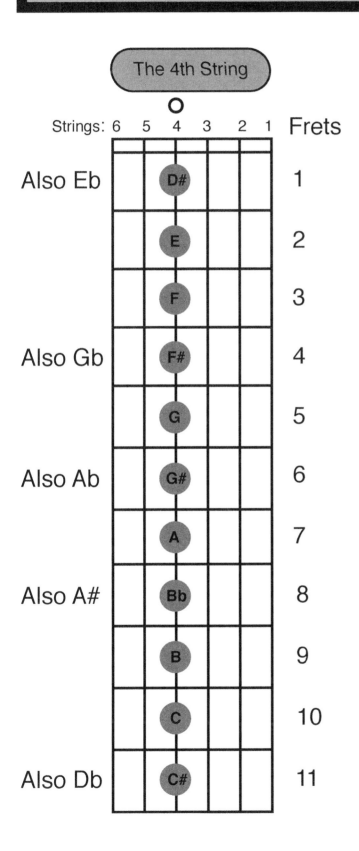

Strings: 6 5 4 3 2 1	Frets
Also Eb — D#	1
E	2
F	3
Also Gb — F#	4
G	5
Also Ab — G#	6
A	7
Also A# — Bb	8
B	9
C	10
Also Db — C#	11

Notes on the 4th String

+ Let's follow the format of lesson 71: Notes on the 3rd String.

+ If you play the 4th String, (marked with a O in the 4th-String Chart on the right of this page), the note "D" will sound.

+ If you put a finger on the 1st fret of the 4th String, the note "D#" will sound.

+ If you place your 1st finger on the 2nd fret of the 4th String, the note "E" will sound.

+ Try placing a finger on the 5th fret of the 4th String. This is the note "G".

+ Play the 3rd String open (letting the string vibrate). This is the note "G". Now try, once again, playing the 5th fret of the 4th String. This is also a "G". They are the same notes, although on different strings. There are many similar examples of this on the guitar: the same note on different strings.

+ Try placing a finger on the 7th fret of the 4th String. This is the note "A".

+ **Look at the chart on the right and try to find the notes on the 4th string of your guitar neck.**

Lesson 76: 3-Note Moveable Major Chords from the 4th String

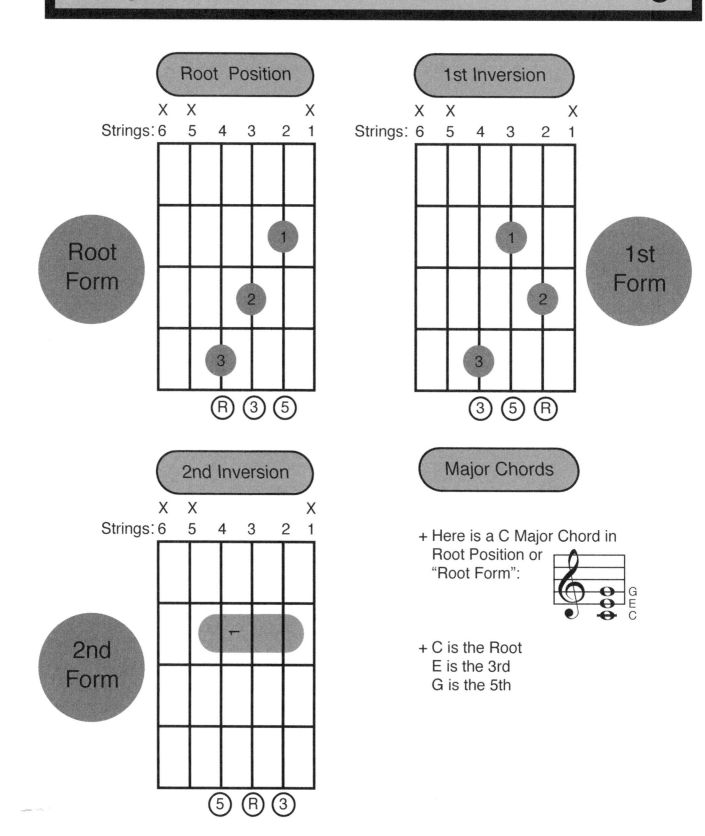

Root Position

Strings: X X   X
6 5 4 3 2 1

Root Form

1
2
3

Ⓡ ③ ⑤

1st Inversion

Strings: X X   X
6 5 4 3 2 1

1st Form

1
2
3

③ ⑤ Ⓡ

2nd Inversion

Strings: X X   X
6 5 4 3 2 1

2nd Form

1

⑤ Ⓡ ③

Major Chords

+ Here is a C Major Chord in Root Position or "Root Form":

G
E
C

+ C is the Root
E is the 3rd
G is the 5th

Lesson 77:
When the Saints Go Marching In

(Place Index Finger
on the Fret Indicated)

Fret:		3rd	3rd	3rd
Form:		Root	Root	Root
Chord:	(No Chord)	G	G	G
	Oh When the	Saints	go marchin' in	
Strum:	1 2 3 4	1 2 3 4	1 2 3 4	1 2 3 4

Fret:	3rd	3rd	3rd	2nd
Form:	Root	Root	Root	1st
Chord:	G	G	G	D
	Oh When the	Saints go	marchin'	in
Strum:	1 2 3 4	1 2 3 4	1 2 3 4	1 2 3 4

Fret:	2nd	3rd	3rd	5th
Form:	1st	Root	Root	2nd
Chord:	D	G	G	C
	Oh Lord, I	want to	be in that	number
Strum:	1 2 3 4	1 2 3 4	1 2 3 4	1 2 3 4

Fret:	5th	3rd	2nd	3rd
Form:	2nd	Root	1st	Root
Chord:	C	G	D	G
	Oh When the	Saints go	marchin'	in
Strum:	1 2 3 4	1 2 3 4	1 2 3 4	1 2 3 4

Chords for "When the Saints Go Marchin' In":

G Major Root Form: Make sure that your index finger is on the 3rd Fret of the 2nd String. This will put your left hand in the correct place on the guitar neck.

D Major 1st Form: Make sure that your index finger is on the 2nd Fret of the 3rd String. This will put your left hand in the correct place on the guitar neck.

C Major: Make sure that your index finger forms a barre across the 5th Fret of the 4th, 3rd, and 2nd Strings. This will put your left hand in the correct position.

Lesson 78: Secret to Guitar Success #8: Have Confidence in Your Musicality

One of the most important aspects to your sound and musicality is confidence. Without it your playing will be anemic and bloodless. So, even from the beginning of your journey with the guitar, cultivate an attitude of assurance and grace. Your confidence does not need to be loud and brash (although that is fine, if that's your musical personality); it can also be solid and quietly strong.

One of the best ways to build your confidence with the guitar is to get out and play with people. Little by little, you and your friends may form a band and play gigs around your town. The more that you do this, the easier it will be to get up in front of of a crowd. For most guitarists, performing is a skill that needs to be developed (just like learning chords, licks, and scales). So, the step now would be to learn some songs, start playing them with friends, and, then, set up some gigs (most likely for free) at your school, local coffee shop, religious institution, etc. This is what it is all about after all.

Lesson 79: Secret to Guitar Success #9: Develop Your Own Musical Voice

In the end, wherever your guitar playing takes you, the most vital aspect of your musicality is the development of your own artist voice. This is an ongoing, lifelong process and it is composed of many elements ranging from your musical influences, the books you have read, your favorite foods, your life experiences (from the monumental to the seemingly trivial), and the musicians with whom you create music. Over time, your musical voice will evolve, based on all of these influences and perceptions. You should be open to these developments, because having music in your life--however big or small--gives it a sense of adventure.

This book and video course is only a starting point for your Rock guitar playing. I hope that it has been helpful in giving you insights and solid foundation into techniques, licks, and some basic music theory used in Rock styles. All of the licks and techniques presented should serve as springboards to your own playing and the development of your musical voice; so, feel free to explore each one and create variations based on your own expression. Of all of these "secrets" to guitar success, the first and last (numbers one and eleven) are the most important: Cultivate a positive attitude in your music making and develop your musical voice.

Lesson 80: Power Chords

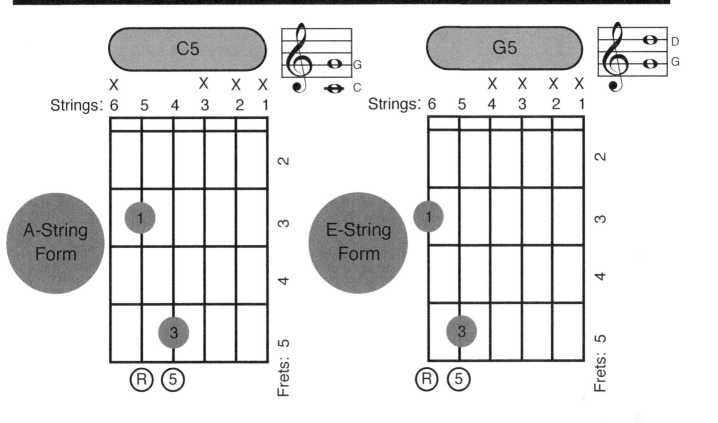

- Power Chords, in general, are 2-note chords that are used in guitar-oriented music that has a driving beat.

- Power Chords are made up of the Root and 5th of the chord. The 3rd of the chord is usually not played.

- The two chords depicted above are the most common forms of power chords. These forms can be moved up and down the neck just like the other moveable chord forms found in this book.

Lesson 81: Power Chords, Part 2 & *Rock Progression*

• As you strum these chords, try gently placing your right-hand palm on top of the strings. This will dampen the sound and change its character.

• Try strumming the power chords in the first line <u>without</u> palm muting and in the second line <u>with</u> palm muting.

• Try strumming beats 1 and 2 (the first two beats of each measure) with palm muting. Then, lift your right hand up and play beats 3 and 4 (the last two beats of each measure) without palm muting.

• Experiment with different combinations of palm muting.

Index Finger on the 3rd Fret

Chord: C5	C5	G5	G5
Strum: 1 2 3 4	1 2 3 4	1 2 3 4	1 2 3 4

Chord: C5	C5	G5	G5
Strum: 1 2 3 4	1 2 3 4	1 2 3 4	1 2 3 4

Lesson 82: 3-Note Moveable Minor Chords from the 3rd String

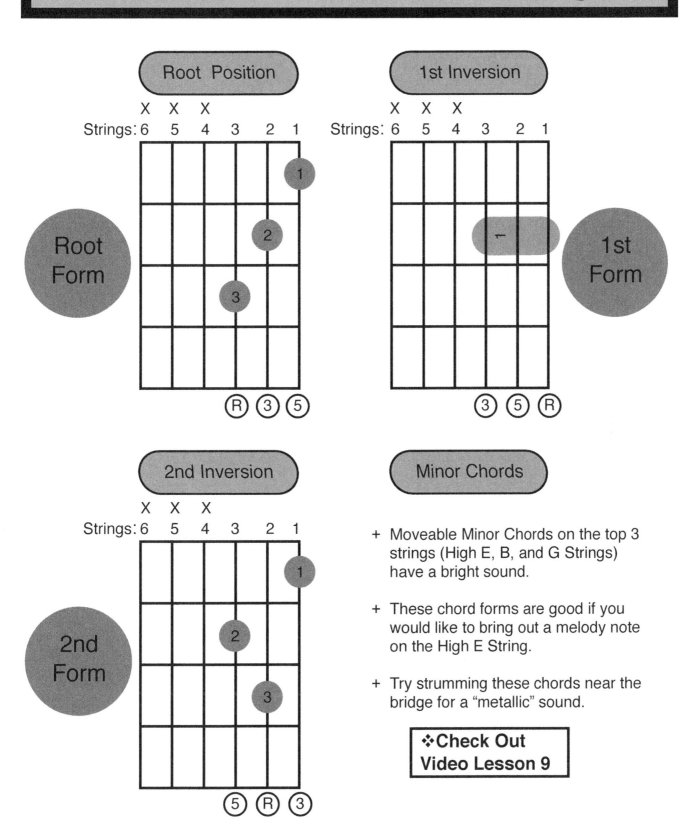

Root Position

X X X
Strings: 6 5 4 3 2 1

Root Form

1
2
3

Ⓡ ③ ⑤

1st Inversion

X X X
Strings: 6 5 4 3 2 1

1st Form

1

③ ⑤ Ⓡ

2nd Inversion

X X X
Strings: 6 5 4 3 2 1

2nd Form

1
2
3

⑤ Ⓡ ③

Minor Chords

+ Moveable Minor Chords on the top 3 strings (High E, B, and G Strings) have a bright sound.

+ These chord forms are good if you would like to bring out a melody note on the High E String.

+ Try strumming these chords near the bridge for a "metallic" sound.

❖Check Out
Video Lesson 9

Lesson 83: Funk- & Reggae-Style Chords

- To create a Funk-Style strumming pattern, strum an up / down pattern twice, very fast, using the

1st Form

- To create a Reggae-Style strumming pattern, palm mute the 1st & 3rd beats and do up-strums on the 2nd and 4th beats.
- M = Mute
- ↑ = Up-strum pattern

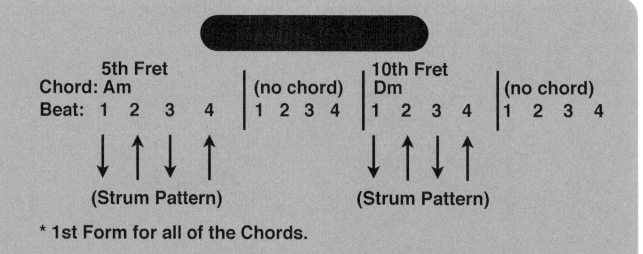

	5th Fret				(no chord)				10th Fret				(no chord)			
Chord:	Am								Dm							
Beat:	1	2	3	4	1	2	3	4	1	2	3	4	1	2	3	4
	↓	↑	↓	↑					↓	↑	↓	↑				

(Strum Pattern)   (Strum Pattern)

* 1st Form for all of the Chords.

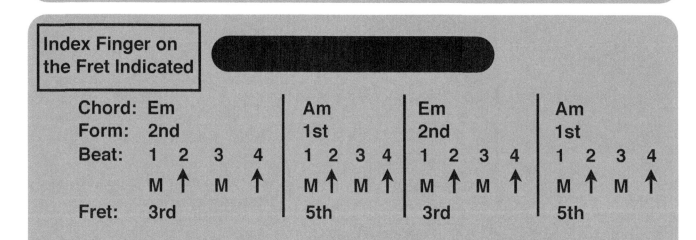

Index Finger on the Fret Indicated

Chord:	Em				Am				Em				Am			
Form:	2nd				1st				2nd				1st			
Beat:	1	2	3	4	1	2	3	4	1	2	3	4	1	2	3	4
	M	↑	M	↑	M	↑	M	↑	M	↑	M	↑	M	↑	M	↑
Fret:	3rd				5th				3rd				5th			

Lesson 84: 3-Note Moveable Minor Chords from the 4th String

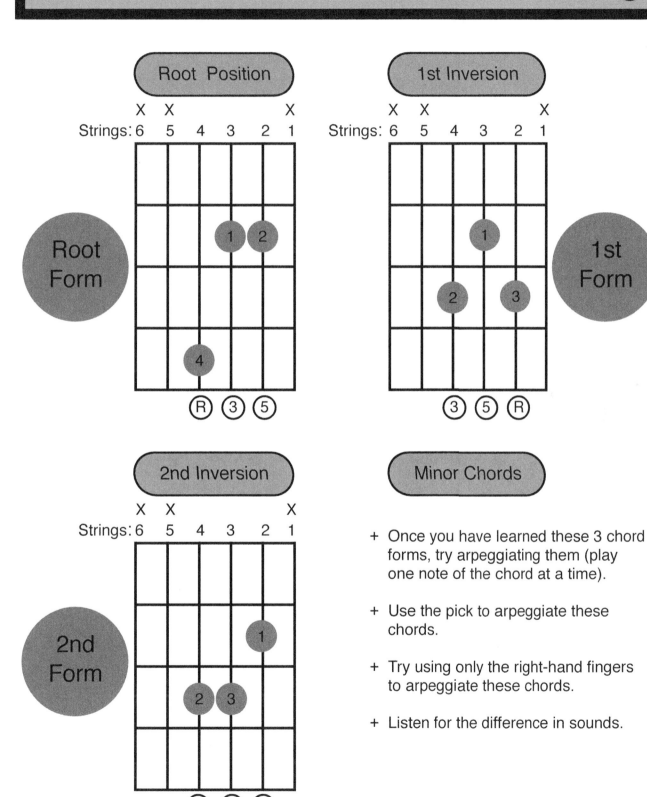

Root Position

Strings: 6 5 4 3 2 1

Root Form

1st Inversion

Strings: 6 5 4 3 2 1

1st Form

2nd Inversion

Strings: 6 5 4 3 2 1

2nd Form

Minor Chords

+ Once you have learned these 3 chord forms, try arpeggiating them (play one note of the chord at a time).

+ Use the pick to arpeggiate these chords.

+ Try using only the right-hand fingers to arpeggiate these chords.

+ Listen for the difference in sounds.

Lesson 85: Contrasting Moveable & Open Position Chords

To create variety in songs, try alternating between moveable and open position chords.

- In *House of the Rising Sun,* try strumming 1st-Form Moveable Chords for the Minor Chords in lines 1 & 2. For the Major Chords in lines 1 & 2, use the 2nd-Form Major Chords from Lesson 76. Then, for lines 3 & 4, try strumming Open Position Chords. Listen for the difference in sounds between these two chord forms.
- Next, try sliding into the Moveable Chords from one fret below. For example, for the C Chord in measure 2, slide from the 4th to the 5th fret.

* From Lesson 76											Index Finger on the Fret Indicated	
Moveable Chord:	Am			C			D			F		
Fret:	9th			5th*			7th*			10th*		
Beat:	1	2	3	1	2	3	1	2	3	1	2	3
Moveable Chord:	Am			C			E			E		
Fret:	9th			5th*			9th*			9th*		
Beat:	1	2	3	1	2	3	1	2	3	1	2	3
Open Chord:	Am			C			D			F		
Beat:	1	2	3	1	2	3	1	2	3	1	2	3
Open Chord:	Am			E			Am			Am		
Beat:	1	2	3	1	2	3	1	2	3	1	2	3

Lesson 86:
Major Barre Chords

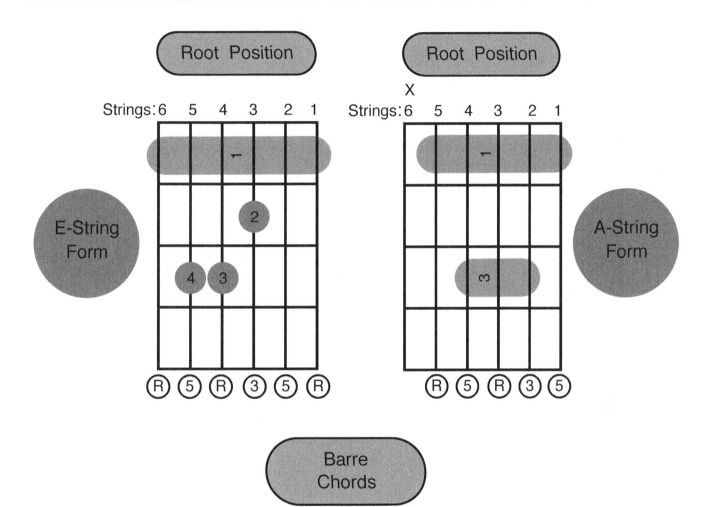

• For Barre Chords, the Index Finger (Finger Number 1) is placed over 5 or 6 Strings.
• These Chords are very helpful, since they are full-sounding, Moveable Chords.
• They do require a fair amount of finger strength.
• So, take your time in practicing them.
• It is best to start with the index finger "clamp" and then gradually add the notes of the chord.

Lesson 87: *Peace Like a River* using Major Barre Chords

Barre-Chord Positions for *Peace Like a River*

E-String Forms:

- **A** : Index finger on the 5th Fret
- **B** : Index finger on the 7th Fret
- **E** : Open Position (no Barre Chord)

A-String Forms:

- **A** : Open Position (no Barre Chord)
- **B** : Index finger on the 2nd Fret
- **E** : Index finger on the 7th Fret

Chord: (No Chord)	E	E	A
I've got	peace like a	river. I've got	Peace like a
Strum: 1 2 3 4	1 2 3 4	1 2 3 4	1 2 3 4

Chord: E	E	E	B
river. I've got	peace like a	river in my	soul.
Strum: 1 2 3 4	1 2 3 4	1 2 3 4	1 2 3 4

Chord: B	E	E	A
I've got	Peace like a	river. I've got	peace like a
Strum: 1 2 3 4	1 2 3 4	1 2 3 4	1 2 3 4

Chord: E	E	B	E
river. I've got	peace like a	river in my	soul.
Strum: 1 2 3 4	1 2 3 4	1 2 3 4	1 2 3 4

Lesson 88: Minor Barre Chords

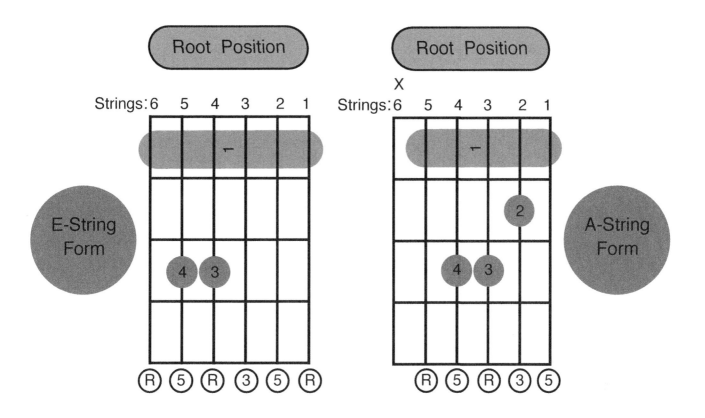

Root Position   Root Position

E-String Form   A-String Form

- For Minor Barre Chords, the Index Finger (Finger Number 1) is placed over 5 or 6 Strings.
- These Chords are very similar to the Major Barre Chord forms.
- The most common forms (shown above) are on the 6th and 5th Strings.
- Like the Major Barre Chord forms, they also require a bit of finger strength. So, take your time in practicing them.
- It is best to start with the index finger "clamp" and then gradually add the notes of the chord.

Lesson 89: *House of the Rising Sun* Using Barre Chords

Barre-Chord Positions for *House of the Rising Sun*

E-String Forms:

    Am: Index finger on the 5th Fret
    C : Index finger on the 8th Fret
    D : Index finger on the 10th Fret
    F : Index finger on the 1st Fret
    E : Open Position (no Barre Chord)

A-String Forms:

    Am: Open Position (no Barre Chord)
    C : Index finger on the 3rd Fret
    D : Index finger on the 5th Fret
    F : Index finger on the 8th Fret
    E : Index finger on the 7th Fret

Chord:	Am	C	D	F
	There is a	house in	New Or-	leans they
Strum:	1 2 3	1 2 3	1 2 3	1 2 3

Chord:	Am	C	E	E
	call the	ris- ing	sun.	It's
Strum:	1 2 3	1 2 3	1 2 3	1 2 3

Chord:	Am	C	D	F
	been the	ruin of	many poor	souls and
Strum:	1 2 3	1 2 3	1 2 3	1 2 3

Chord:	Am	E	Am	Am
	Lord, I	know I'm	one.	
Strum:	1 2 3	1 2 3	1 2 3	1 2 3

Lesson 90: *House of the Rising Sun* Using Power Chords

Power-Chord Positions for *House of the Rising*

E-String Forms: Strum only the 5th and 6th Strings

    Am: Index finger on the 5th Fret
    C : Index finger on the 8th Fret
    D : Index finger on the 10th Fret
    F : Index finger on the 1st Fret
    E : Open Position (Index finger on the 2nd fret of the 5th String)

A-String Forms: Strum only the 4th and 5th Strings

    Am: Open Position (Index finger on the 2nd fret of the 4th String)
    C : Index finger on the 3rd Fret
    D : Index finger on the 5th Fret
    F : Index finger on the 8th Fret
    E : Index finger on the 7th Fret

Chord:	Am	C	D	F
	There is a	house in	New Or-	leans they
Strum:	1 2 3	1 2 3	1 2 3	1 2 3

Chord:	Am	C	E	E
	call the	ris- ing	sun.	It's
Strum:	1 2 3	1 2 3	1 2 3	1 2 3

Chord:	Am	C	D	F
	been the	ruin of	many poor	souls and
Strum:	1 2 3	1 2 3	1 2 3	1 2 3

Chord:	Am	E	Am	Am
	Lord, I	know I'm	one.	
Strum:	1 2 3	1 2 3	1 2 3	1 2 3

Lesson 91:
Dominant 7th Barre Chords

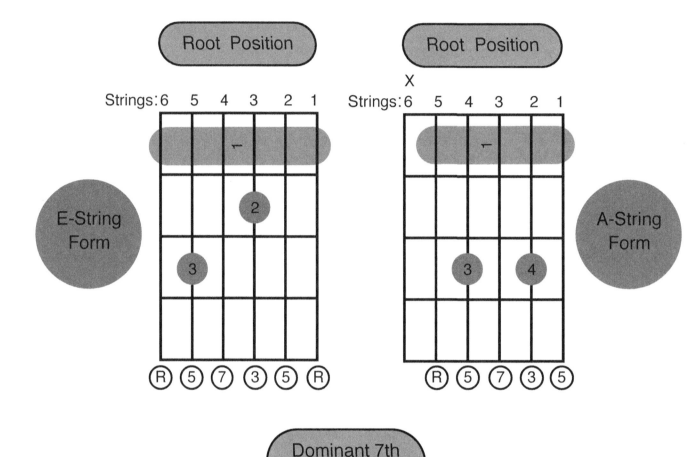

Root Position

Root Position

E-String Form

A-String Form

Dominant 7th Barre Chords

- For Dominant 7th Barre Chords, the Index Finger is placed over 5 or 6 Strings.
- These Chords are very helpful, since they are full-sounding, Moveable Chords.
- The E-String Form has a similar shape to the open E7 chord from Lesson 48.
- The A-String Form has a similar shape to the open A7 chord, also from Lesson 48.

Lesson 92: *Amazing Grace* Using Dominant 7 Barre Chords

Fret:	5th	5th	3rd	5th
Form:	A-String	A-String	E-String	A-String
Chord:	D7	D7	G7	D7
	A-mazing	Grace how	sweet the	sound that
Strum:	1 2 3	1 2 3	1 2 3	1 2 3

Fret:	5th	5th	5th	5th
Form:	A-String	A-String	E-String	E-String
Chord:	D7	D7	A7	A7
	saved a	wretch like	me.	I
Strum:	1 2 3	1 2 3	1 2 3	1 2 3

Fret:	5th	5th	3rd	5th
Form:	A-String	A-String	E-String	A-String
Chord:	D7	D7	G7	D7
	once was	lost but	now am	found. Was
Strum:	1 2 3	1 2 3	1 2 3	1 2 3

Fret:	5th	5th	5th	5th
Form:	A-String	E-String	A-String	A-String
Chord:	D7	A7	D7	D7
	blind but	now I	see.	
Strum:	1 2 3	1 2 3	1 2 3	1 2 3

Lesson 93: *12-Bar Blues with Dominant 7th Barre Chords*

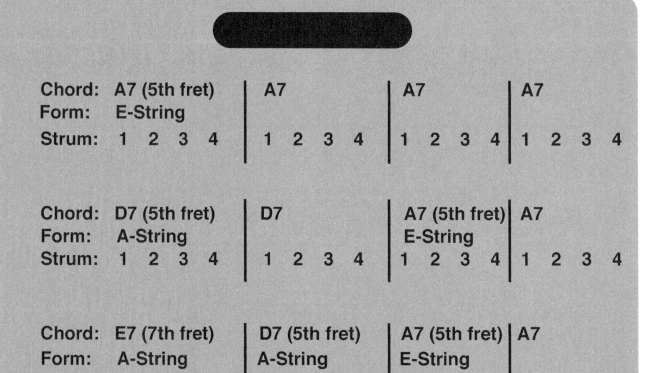

Chord:	A7 (5th fret)	A7	A7	A7
Form:	E-String			
Strum:	1 2 3 4	1 2 3 4	1 2 3 4	1 2 3 4

Chord:	D7 (5th fret)	D7	A7 (5th fret)	A7
Form:	A-String		E-String	
Strum:	1 2 3 4	1 2 3 4	1 2 3 4	1 2 3 4

Chord:	E7 (7th fret)	D7 (5th fret)	A7 (5th fret)	A7
Form:	A-String	A-String	E-String	
Strum:	1 2 3 4	1 2 3 4	1 2 3 4	1 2 3 4

Fretboard Positions for *12-Bar Blues*

A7: E-String Form on the 5th Fret

D7: A-String Form on the 5th Fret

E7: A-String Form on the 7th Fret

Lesson 94:
Minor 7th Barre Chords

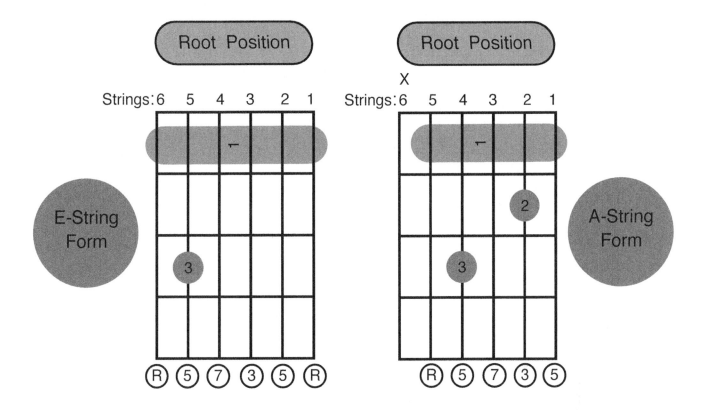

E-String Form

Root Position

Strings: 6 5 4 3 2 1

1

3

R 5 7 3 5 R

Root Position

X

Strings: 6 5 4 3 2 1

1

2

3

R 5 7 3 5

A-String Form

Minor 7th Barre Chords

- For Minor 7th Barre Chords, the Index Finger is placed over 5 or 6 Strings.
- These Chords are very helpful, since they are full-sounding, Moveable Chords.
- The E-String Form has a similar shape to the open Em7 chord from Lesson 62.
- The A-String Form has a similar shape to the open Am7 chord, also from Lesson 62.

Lesson 95: *Jazz Minor Blues* Using Minor 7th Barre Chords

in A minor

Chord:	Am7				Am7				Dm7				Am7			
	Sometimes I				feel	like a			motherless				child.			
Strum:	1	2	3	4	1	2	3	4	1	2	3	4	1	2	3	4

Chord:	Dm7				Dm7				E7				Am7			
	Sometimes I				feel	like a			motherless				child.			
Strum:	1	2	3	4	1	2	3	4	1	2	3	4	1	2	3	4

Chord:	Am7				Am7				Dm7				Am7			
	Sometimes I				feel	like a			motherless				child.			A-
Strum:	1	2	3	4	1	2	3	4	1	2	3	4	1	2	3	4

Chord:	F				Am7				E7				Am7			
	long				way		from	home.								A-
Strum:	1	2	3	4	1	2	3	4	1	2	3	4	1	2	3	4

Chord:	F				Am7				E7				Am7			
	long				way		from	home.								
Strum:	1	2	3	4	1	2	3	4	1	2	3	4	1	2	3	4

Fretboard Positions for the E-String Barre-Chord Forms

Am7: 5th Fret
Dm7: 10th Fret
E7: Open Position
F: 1st Fret

Lesson 96: *When the Saints with 7th Barre Chords*

Fret:	3rd	3rd	3rd
Form:	E-String		
Chord: (No Chord)	G7	G7	G7
Oh When the	Saints	go marchin'	in
Strum: 1 2 3 4	1 2 3 4	1 2 3 4	1 2 3 4

Fret: 3rd	3rd	3rd	5th
Form: E-String			A-String
Chord: G7	G7	G7	D7
Oh When the	Saints go	marchin'	in
Strum: 1 2 3 4	1 2 3 4	1 2 3 4	1 2 3 4

Fret: 5th	3rd	3rd	3rd
Form: A-String	E-String	E-String	A-String
Chord: D7	G7	G7	C7
Oh Lord, I	want to	be in that	number
Strum: 1 2 3 4	1 2 3 4	1 2 3 4	1 2 3 4

Fret: 3rd	3rd	5th	3rd
Form: A-String	E-String	A-String	E-String
Chord: C7	G7	D7	G7
Oh When the	Saints go	marchin'	in
Strum: 1 2 3 4	1 2 3 4	1 2 3 4	1 2 3 4

Try strumming the chords with the back side of the pick or with your thumb for a different sound.

Lesson 97
Major 7th Chords: Open Position

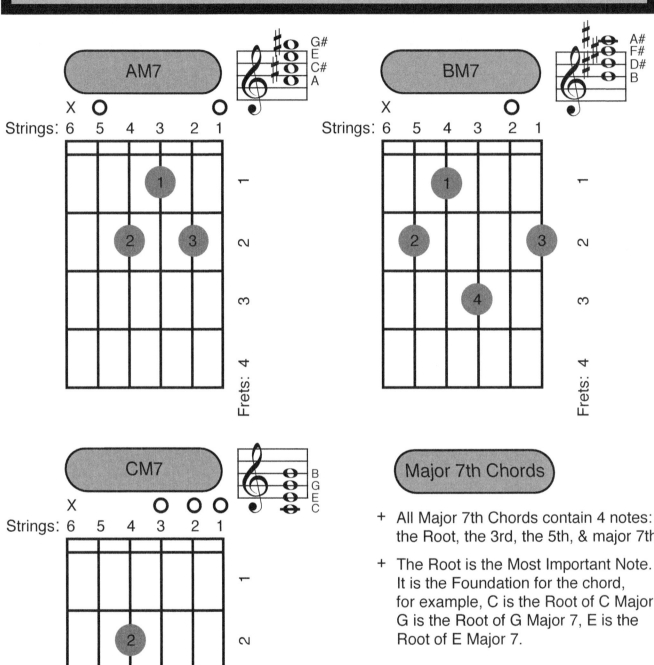

AM7

Strings: 6 5 4 3 2 1

BM7

Strings: 6 5 4 3 2 1

CM7

Strings: 6 5 4 3 2 1

Major 7th Chords

+ All Major 7th Chords contain 4 notes: the Root, the 3rd, the 5th, & major 7th.

+ The Root is the Most Important Note. It is the Foundation for the chord, for example, C is the Root of C Major 7, G is the Root of G Major 7, E is the Root of E Major 7.

+ Major 7th Chords are often abbreviated with the Chord Letter, a Capital M, and the Number 7. For example, AM7 and DM7 stand for A Major Seventh Chord and D Major Seventh Chord.

+ Major 7th Chords have a "jazzy" quality and can "spice" up Major Chords.

Lesson 98
Major 7th Chords: Open Position

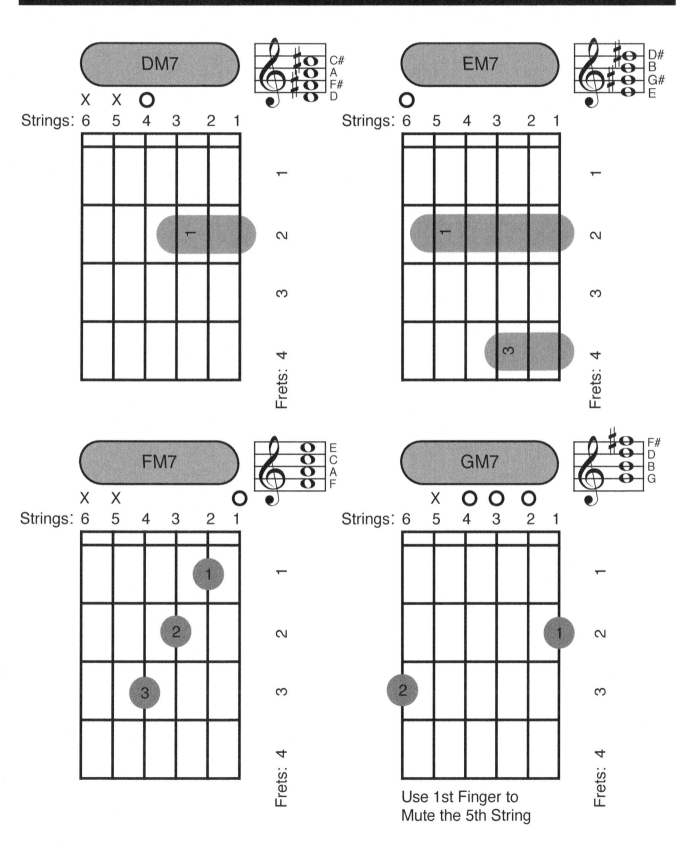

Lesson 99
Major 7th Chords: Open Position

Chord: CM7	CM7	FM7	FM7
Strum: 1 2 3 4	1 2 3 4	1 2 3 4	1 2 3 4

Chord: DM7	DM7	AM7	AM7
Strum: 1 2 3 4	1 2 3 4	1 2 3 4	1 2 3 4

Chord: EM7	EM7	BM7	BM7
Strum: 1 2 3 4	1 2 3 4	1 2 3 4	1 2 3 4

Chord: GM7	GM7	CM7	CM7
Strum: 1 2 3 4	1 2 3 4	1 2 3 4	1 2 3 4

Try playing this song at different tempi (speeds):

1. A slow tempo

2. A Moderate tempo

3. A Fast tempo

Lesson 100:
Moveable Augmented Chords

Overview

+ Augmented Chords are more "advanced" than Major and Minor Chords.

+ They are based on two sets of major-third intervals.

+ Augmented Chords are often used as transitional chords between two more significant chords in a song.

+ They embellish the harmony and make more colorful progressions.

+ We go into more detail for Augmented Chords in the *Ultimate Guitar Scales, Chords & Arpeggios Handbook.* **Check it out to take your playing to the next level!**

Augmented Chords

+ All Augmented Chords contain 3 notes: the Root, the 3rd, and the 5th.

+ In Augmented Chords the distance between the Root and the 3rd is made up of 2 Major 2nds

+ In Augmented Chords the distance between the 3rd and the 5th is also made up of 2 Major 2nds

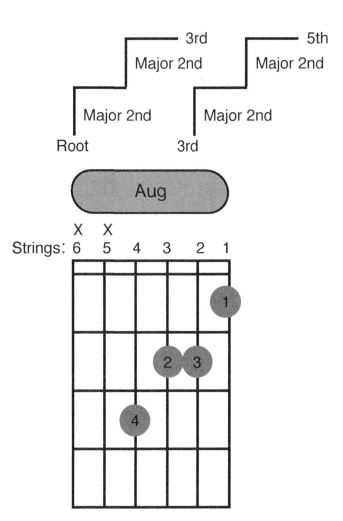

Aug

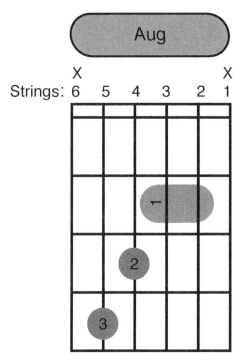

Strings: 6 5 4 3 2 1

Aug

Strings: 6 5 4 3 2 1

Lesson 101:
Moveable Diminished Chords

Overview

+ Diminished Chords are more "advanced" than Major and Minor Chords.

+ They are based on two sets of minor-third intervals.

+ Diminished Chords are often used as transitional chords between two more significant chords in a song.

+ They embellish chord progressions and give them a little bit more musical "spice" and expressivity.

Diminished Chords

+ All Diminished Chords contain 3 notes: the Root, the 3rd, and the 5th.

+ In Diminished Chords the distance between the Root and the 3rd is made up of 1 Major 2nd and 1 Minor 2nd.

+ In Diminished Chords the distance between the 3rd and the 5th is also made up of 1 Major 2nd and 1 Minor 2nd.

Diminished Chord Intervals

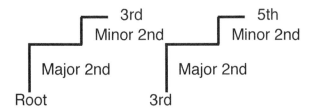

Dim

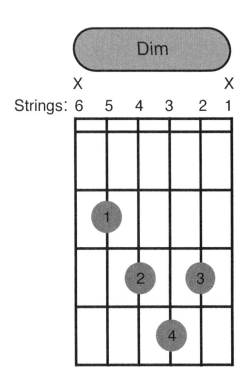

Congratulations on finishing the book! You have learned a great number of creative and practical concepts and techniques for the guitar. We hope that you enjoyed this book and video course. We are always happy to hear from our readers! Please feel free to reach out to us at steeplechasemusic.com.

Keep up the good work!

Lesson 102:
Red River Valley

Lesson 103:
Aura Lee

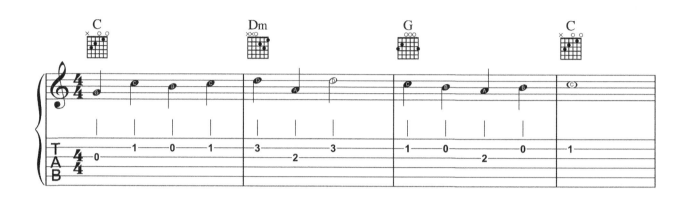

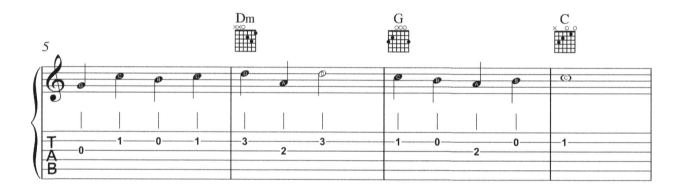

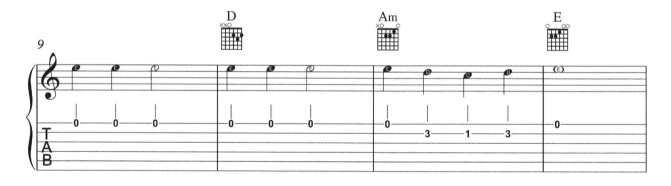

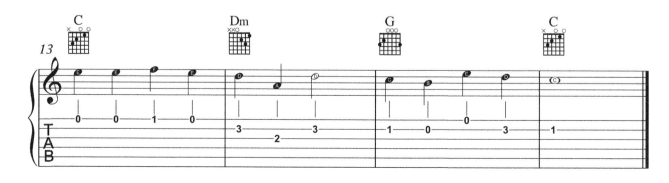

Lesson 104:
Happy Birthday

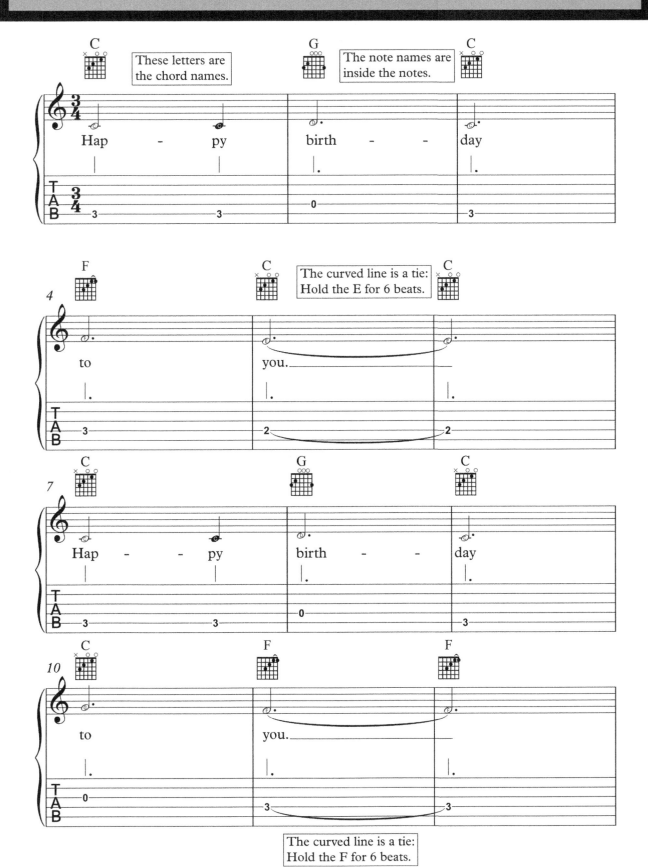

These letters are the chord names.

The note names are inside the notes.

The curved line is a tie: Hold the E for 6 beats.

The curved line is a tie: Hold the F for 6 beats.

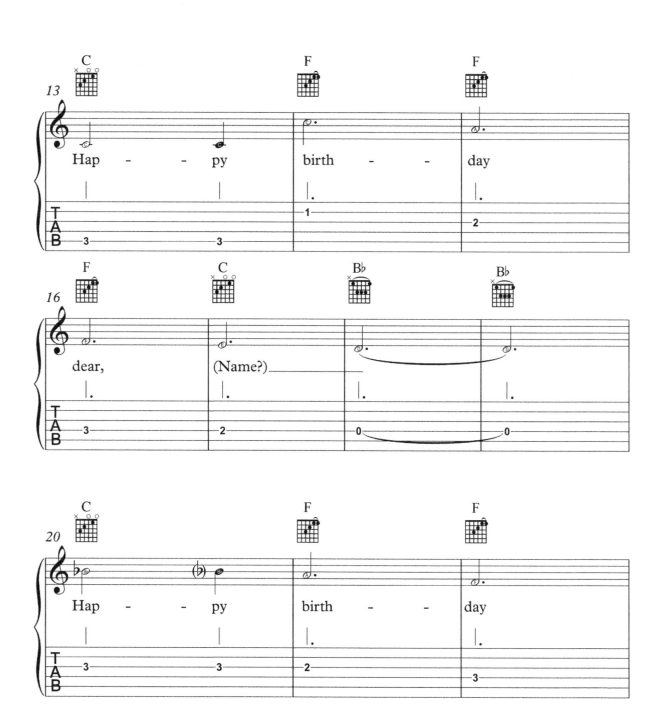

Lesson 105:
Shenandoah

Lesson 106:
Silent Night

Lesson 107:
This Little Light of Mine

Suggestions for Listening:

A Short (and incomplete) List of Guitarists who have an imaginative approach to chords

Jimi Hendrix

The Edge

Eric Johnson

Alan Holdsworth

Pete Townshend

Mark Knopfler

Wes Montgomery

Eddie Van Halen

Joe Pass

Michael Hedges

Tommy Emmanuel

Angus Young

James Hetfield

Robbie Robertson

Steve Morse

About the Author

Damon Ferrante is a composer, guitarist, and music writer. When he was 8 years old, his uncle left an old electric guitar, which was in two pieces (neck and body separated) at his parents' house. Damon put the guitar together using some old screws and duct tape. That was the beginning of a wild ride through Rock, Jazz, Classical Music, and Opera that has spanned over 20 years. Along the way, Ferrante has had performances at Carnegie Hall, Symphony Space, and throughout the US and Europe. He has taught on the music faculties of Seton Hall University and Montclair State University. He is the director of Steeplechase Arts, a music production and publishing company that he founded in 2003.

Acknowledgements

I am grateful to the many people who helped in the design and editing process for this book: Noah Engel and Jackson Highland-Lipski for their excellent video and photo work, Ba for her design advice, Jason Ferrante for his insights into lesson planning, Amy and David for their tech assistance, Barbara and Joe for everything else.

Dedication

This book is dedicated to the hundreds of students, over the last two decades, who have helped teach me how to play the guitar. Here is a short list: Baird and Gabe Acheson, Theo Epstein, Caleb and Josh Brooks, Teddy and Charlie Obrecht, Gabriel and Bridget Donner, Tom, Lauren, and Kim Riley, Hannah and Emma Pope, Alex and Mika Poblete, Will and Ben Gantt, Ty and Will Washburn, David and Andrew Brennan, Ylva Hellstrand, Stephan Dalal, Cyrus Alamzad, Amanda, Olivia and Kyle Shattuck, Annabelle Hu, Skyler Snow, Jasper and Teddy Martin, and Jack and Sophia Algerio.

Take Your Guitar Playing to the Next Level!

Guitar Scales Handbook

A Step-By-Step, 100-Lesson Guide to Scales, Music Theory, and
Fretboard Theory (Book & Videos)
Damon Ferrante

Learn Piano!

Piano Scales Chords
Arpeggios Lessons

Book & Videos   Damon Ferrante

Piano Book for Adult Beginners

Teach Yourself How to Play Famous Piano Songs, Read Music, Theory & Technique

No Music Reading Required!

Damon Ferrante

Book & Streaming Video Lessons

We want to help you become the guitarist of your dreams!

Check Out Steeplechasemusic.com for Free Guitar Lessons in Your Inbox!

Printed in Great Britain
by Amazon

71269706R00072